MW00633330

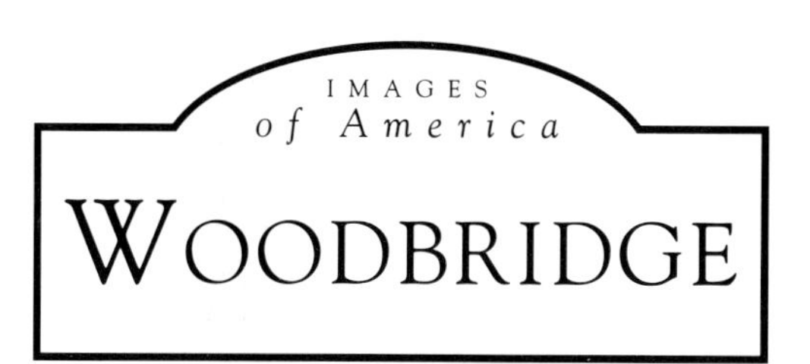
IMAGES
of America
WOODBRIDGE

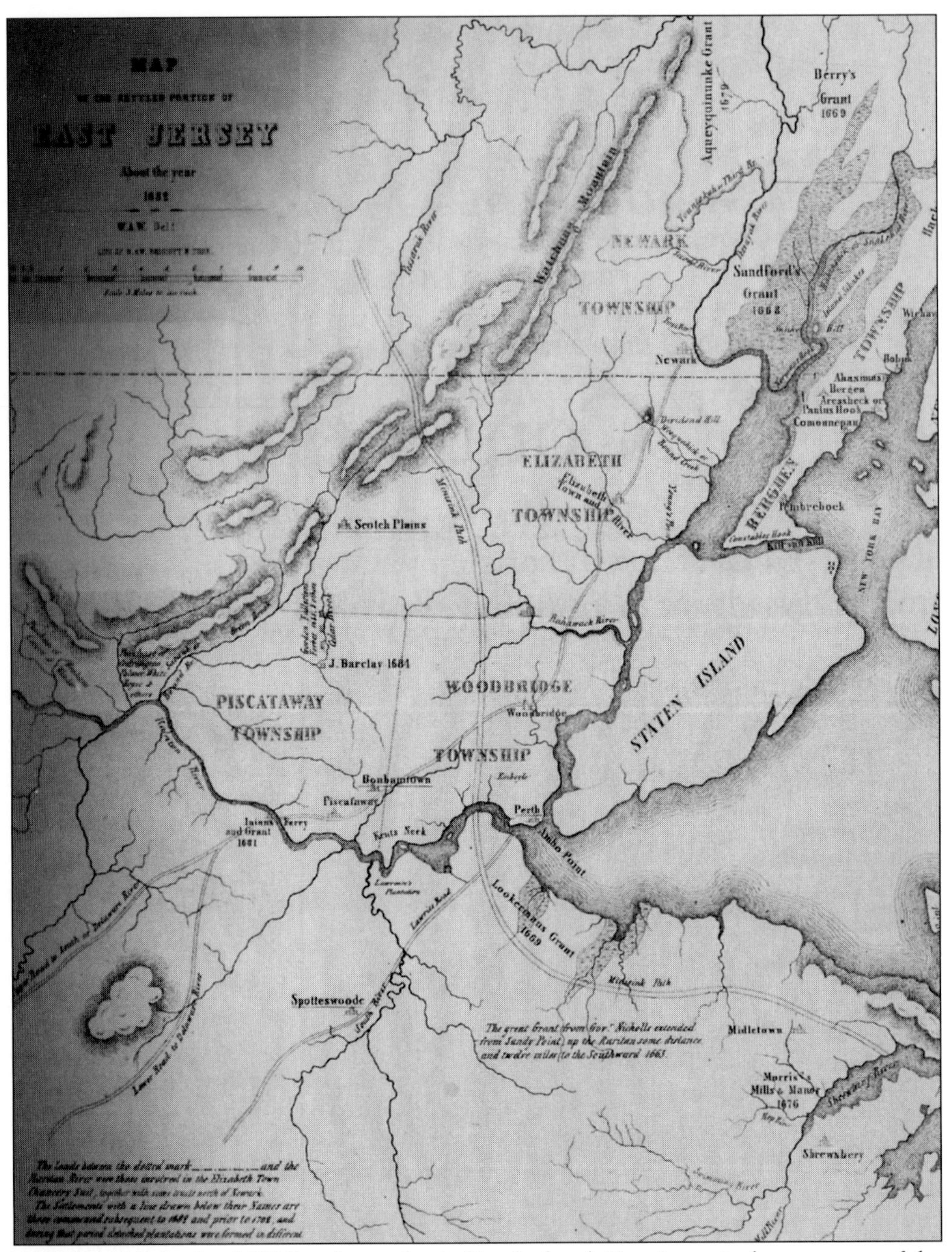

EARLY MAP. In this 1656 Dutch map by A. Vanderdonck New Jersey is shown as part of the New Netherlands. Woodbridge would be settled on land north of the Raritan River at the time the English took control of the Dutch territories in 1664. (Images of America: *Scotch Plains and Fanwood*)

COVER: Veteran's Drum Corps, *c.* 1900. See page 20 for further information.

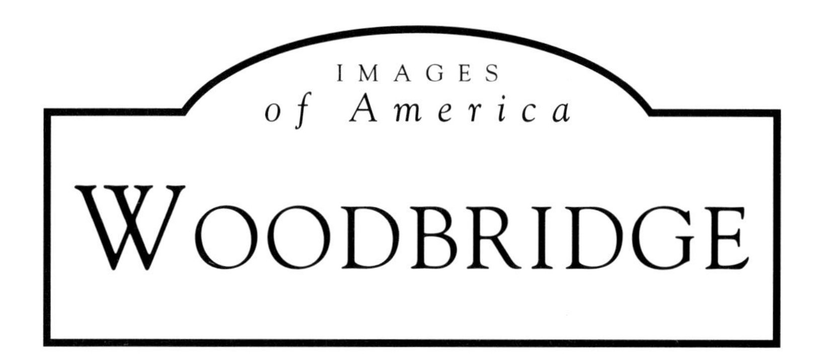

Robert J. McEwen and Virginia Bergen Troeger

First published 1997

ISBN 0-7524-0561-6

Published by Arcadia Publishing,
an imprint of the Chalford Publishing Corporation,
One Washington Center, Dover, New Hampshire 03820.
Printed in Great Britain

Library of Congress Cataloging-in-Publication Data applied for

To the memory of my mother, Thora Louise Thomsen McEwen (1893–1990),
and father, Joseph McEwen (1888–1961),
lifelong residents of Woodbridge,
whose memories would have included many of the scenes in this book.
R.J.McE.

To the memory of my mother and father,
Miriam Duval Bergen and Albert Roll Bergen,
who were residents of West Main Street, Woodbridge, for many years.
V.B.T.

AUTHOR'S NOTE: Unless otherwise noted under the photograph, all images are taken from the collection of Robert J. McEwen.

Contents

Introduction

The Township of Woodbridge in Middlesex County has been a settled community in the state of New Jersey for more than three hundred years. In 1664 the English took control of New Netherlands from the Dutch and divided the area of New Jersey into two sections, East Jersey and West Jersey. When Philip Carteret became governor of East Jersey, he invited New Englanders to move to his province. Puritans from New Hampshire colonized Piscataway, while settlers from Newbery, Massachusetts, established the Township of Woodbridge. At the time that the English granted the official charter for Woodbridge in 1669, the boundaries included Carteret, lower Rahway south of the Rahway River, Oak Tree, New Dover, Bonhamtown, Metuchen, Menlo Park, and the eastern section of Edison.

These early colonists may have named their town for a Newbery clergyman Reverend John Woodbridge or for the town of Woodbridge in Suffolk County, England, the original home of many of the settlers. Or perhaps it was a combination of both.

During the Revolutionary War the British occupied Woodbridge from December 1776 to June 1777. Many Woodbridge residents took an active part in the struggle for independence. Nathaniel Heard commanded the Middlesex County Militia and arrested William Franklin, the last English governor of New Jersey. Nathaniel Fitz Randolph, Samuel F. Parker, Samuel Crow, David Edgar, and many others served as officers in the Continental Army. Janet (or Jennet) Pike Gage, wife of Philip Gage, an English sympathizer, raised the first flagpole or liberty pole in town at the Cross Keys Tavern on Main Street and Amboy Avenue. Janet is buried on the grounds of the Woodbridge Methodist Church on Main Street. Her nephew, Zebulon Montgomery Pike, who spent time in Woodbridge as a child, has been immortalized as the discoverer of Pike's Peak in the Colorado Rocky Mountains.

By the 1890s Woodbridge had emerged as a major clay producing area and manufacturer of superior firebricks, an industry that continued until the 1980s. Many thriving clay mining and firebrick companies opened in town, attracting Irish, German, and later Hungarian immigrants to the area to work.

Although the two major highways built during the 1950s—the New Jersey Turnpike and the Garden State Parkway—go their separate ways, they cross at the Fords section of Woodbridge. This intersection has drawn industry and office complexes to Woodbridge and nearby sections of Middlesex County. Woodbridge experienced a major population growth during the 1960s and is now one of the largest municipalities in the state.

Whatever your age, whatever your relationship to Woodbridge Township, may the past as reflected in these vintage images speak to you in many ways. Perhaps these pages will awaken memories long forgotten, perhaps they will reveal a thread of past history you never knew, or perhaps you'll see a familiar face or place in a new light. But above all, may you find your life enriched and your sense of community strengthened by exploring Images of America: *Woodbridge*.

Acknowledgments

Although compiled by just two people, a book about a large community like Woodbridge involves a great many others behind the scenes. We are indebted to the photographers who took pictures, whatever their reasons were for recording family, friends, familiar scenes, and news events around the Township. And, of course, there are the many people interested in preserving the past who shared their photographs and knowledge of Woodbridge Township with us. Without them our book would not exist.

I would especially like to thank my wife, Betsy, for allowing me to clutter our house with the historic memorabilia and Woodbridge photos used in this book. Also thanks to my co-author, Virginia Bergen Troeger, whose knowledge and interest in Woodbridge history plus her superior writing skills have made this book not just a collection of photos, but an entertaining partial history of Woodbridge Township from the late 1800s to the early 1950s.

I especially want to thank Frank Premako of Acme Studio for his fantastic ability to restore tattered, folded, and faded photographs to near perfect newness. Many thanks also go to the friends who allowed me to copy photographs over the years. Two of them, Emily and Margaret Lee, descendants of the Cutters and Pralls, have provided me with much information about these old respected families.

I would also like to extend my gratitude to my friend, Police Detective Bernie Anderson Sr., who has the finest collection of scenes around Woodbridge during the last seventy-five years and has never hesitated to allow me to copy them. The Reverend Philip Noe Nelson, whose family ties go back to Pre-Revolutionary Woodbridge, has shared many family photos and stories, as did Kathy Jost Keating, whose historic home may be the oldest in existence in Woodbridge.

Others who patiently answered questions and loaned their family photographs include Don and Emma Aaroe, Barbara Rush Basehart, Barbara Booz, Catherine Clark Burns, W. Atlee Burpee and Co., Herbert Christensen, Andrew Csepcsar, Dick Dunigan, Carol Hila, Todd Howell, Martha Jansen, Dorothy Kauffman, John Kozub, John Kuhlman, Frank LaPenta, Helen and Janet Mawbey, Dorothy Omenhiser McCabe, Middlesex Water Company, Mary Molnar, Pauline O'Connor, Madeline LaPenta Peterson, Robert Rippen, Ray Schneider, Richard C. Schwarz, Betty Stauffer, Dorothy Klein Slotkin, Raymond Stricker, George and Barbara Wyatt, and Al Yurenda.

R.J.McE.

It was a stroke of pure luck that I became acquainted with my co-author, Robert J. McEwen. After compiling Images of America: *Berkeley Heights* I wanted to write a similar book about my childhood hometown of Woodbridge. Through Arcadia, Bob McEwen called me out of the blue. He told me about his large collection of Woodbridge photographs and his extensive knowledge of the Township. We decided almost immediately to collaborate on this book, and the rest, shall we say, is history!

Special recognition must go to my husband, Walter A. Troeger, a licensed professional engineer, who tackled the many technical questions that arose in writing the captions for the photos. His knowledge of trains, trolley cars, firefighting equipment, racing cars, horse-drawn carriages, barges, boats, and the mechanical details of the dumping of coal, the mining of clay, and the moving of churches proved invaluable. He also scrutinized the photographs and proofread the text countless times with a critical eye for detail, accuracy, clarity, and the reality of our publisher's deadline. My thanks also to Joanne Troeger, Janice Troeger Lettieri, Scott Lavender, and Ernie Lettieri. I am grateful to them for their insightful critiques of the manuscript.

V.B.T.

The clay mining and firebrick manufacturing industries which dominated the economy of Woodbridge during the nineteenth and early twentieth centuries are symbolized in the three sections of the Township's official emblem. The crossed shovel and pick represent the tools used to mine clay; the kiln depicts the firing of the bricks; and the ship's steering wheel symbolizes the boats and other vessels which carried the clay and bricks to market.

One

A Walk Down Main Street

FIRST CATHOLIC CHURCH. In 1865 St. James Chapel was located on the south side of Upper Main Street opposite Metuchen Avenue. In 1887 the congregation built a larger church, also called St. James, and converted this chapel into the first St. James School (pictured here in 1900). For many years the section of Main Street west of Amboy Avenue was known as Upper or West Main Street while the business district was called Lower Main Street.

ST. JAMES CHURCH, *c.* 1910. The second St. James Roman Catholic Church which replaced the St. James Chapel (pictured on preceding page) remained on Upper Main Street until 1924. During that year this church made history when it was moved from Upper Main Street to the corner of Amboy Avenue and Grove Street. (See next three photographs.)

SECOND ST. JAMES CHURCH ON THE MOVE, 1924. No ordinary tractors, these! Note the winch on the left rear axle driven by the motor and controlled by the operator. During a move forward, the tractors are prevented from moving by cables behind them which are attached to chains around steel rods in the ground. As the winch rotates the cables, the church is pulled forward a few feet at a time. The underpinnings of the church are then repositioned for the next forward move. Such a labor-intensive project must have taken many weeks to complete.

SECOND ST. JAMES CHURCH SETTLES IN 1924. It was reported at the time that this massive undertaking marked the first time in the United States that a building of this size was moved by tractors instead of horses. This photo appears to be the final location for the church on Amboy Avenue as evidenced by the adjacent house on Grove Street (at right).

ST. JAMES ON AMBOY AVENUE, *c.* 1930. Shortly after the second St. James Church came to rest here, it was joined next door by a new St. James Parochial School, which continues in operation. The church remained here until it was torn down in the 1960s. At that time a third St. James Church seating fifteen hundred people was built one block away at the corner of Amboy Avenue and Main Street where it remains a thriving house of worship.

UPPER MAIN STREET, *c.* 1945. By the end of World War II most of Upper Main Street was filled with residences of various styles. Balga's Tavern (on right), a neighborhood bar, was located at the corner of St. James Avenue. Farther along on the right are the "twin" stucco houses built as mirror images of each other. And across the street the "little house" where the Schultz family lived for many years is still occupied today.

ALBERT R. BERGEN, 1926. Mr. Bergen from South Amboy and his wife Miriam from Philadelphia purchased the property at 167 Upper Main Street from Clara Bedman. Miss Bedman owned most of the acreage on the south side of Main Street one block above Amboy Avenue. Mr. Bergen sits with Bingo on the steps of 249 Grove Street which he and his wife rented while waiting for their new home on Main Street to be built. (Virginia B. Troeger)

HOUSES ON UPPER MAIN, 1927. The newly built Bergen home stands in the center with the Daltons' house to the left. Clara Bedman's homestead is partially visible on the far left. Years earlier Miss Bedman's father maintained a seed growing business here, supplying W. Atlee Burpee and Co., with scarlet sage (salvia) seeds. Through 1969 the Burpee catalog listed "Clara Bedman or Bonfire Scarlet Sage" flower seeds. (Virginia B. Troeger)

SISTERS, MAY 1929. (From left) Upper Main Street residents Ann, Margaret (Peggy), and Helen Dalton pause for a photo on the backyard loveseat of Miriam and Albert Bergen who were next door neighbors. Ann Dalton Woolley worked for many years as a salesperson in Christensen's Department Store and later in Lawrence Jewelers, both on Lower Main Street. (Virginia B. Troeger)

THE DALLY HOUSE, *c*. 1900. For many years this lovely old home stood at the corner of Upper Main Street and Elmwood Avenue. Samuel Dally, born in 1810 in Mutton Hollow off Upper Main Street, probably lived in this house after his marriage. Throughout his years in business, Mr. Dally wore many hats. He worked as a blacksmith's apprentice, a weaver, and farmer. For several winters he sold oysters in New York state and Pennsylvania, and in 1840 he started a butcher business. Mr. Dally made his fortune, however, in the Woodbridge clay market of the 1850s.

DR. IRA THORP SPENCER, *c.* 1950. A prominent and respected medical doctor for more than fifty years, Dr. Spencer maintained his office in his home at 152 Upper Main Street. Born in Martinsville, New Jersey, he received his medical degree in 1893 from the University of Pennsylvania. He was appointed Township physician in 1897, shortly after settling in Woodbridge. Among his many accomplishments, Dr. Spencer helped found the Rahway Memorial Hospital and served as president of the Middlesex County Medical Society.

MAIN STREET NEIGHBORS, JULY 4, 1935. (From left) Anna Ensign Spencer, Madeleine J. Duval, Mrs. Spencer's daughter Elizabeth, Virginia Bergen, Mrs. Duval's daughter Miriam D. Bergen, and Dr. Ira T. Spencer gather in the Spencers' garden on Main Street for a holiday picnic. Elizabeth Spencer taught seventh grade at School No. 11 for many years. (Virginia B. Troeger)

CROSS KEYS TAVERN, *c.* 1900 (ALSO CALLED CROSS AND KEYS INN). Yes, George Washington did spend the night of April 22, 1789, at this historic tavern located at the time on the northwest corner of Main Street and Amboy Avenue! Washington was traveling by stagecoach from Mount Vernon, Virginia, to New York City for his inauguration the following day as the first president of the United States. Washington arrived here with New Jersey Governor William Livingston who lived in Elizabethtown, New Jersey. The Woodbridge Cavalry, commanded by Captain Ichabod Potter, escorted these important visitors to the tavern. A few years earlier, local patriot Janet Pike Gage raised the first liberty pole or flag pole at Cross Keys Tavern to fly the Stars and Stripes for the first time in Woodbridge. When innkeeper John Manning was named the first postmaster of Woodbridge in 1791, the inn became the town's official post office. Marquis de Lafayette, the famous French soldier who helped the American colonists during the Revolutionary War, visited the inn in 1824 on his way to Philadelphia. Years later the inn was moved to upper James Street. Two signs in front of the building recount its glorious past, but Cross Keys Tavern stands virtually unnoticed and forgotten today.

AT THE CROSSROADS, *c.* 1905. Main Street at Amboy Avenue certainly resembled a quiet country scene with not even a horse and carriage in sight to stir up the dusty roads. The Cross Keys Tavern with its distinctive chimneys (right) had not yet been moved to James Street. The building on the far right would later become the Middlesex Hotel, and the silent movie house on the left was probably the first cinema in Woodbridge.

MAIN AND AMBOY, *c.* 1942. What a difference thirty or more years can make! The streets are paved, the Knights of Columbus clubhouse replaces the Cross Keys Tavern, the Middlesex Hotel owned by the Galaida family stands on the right, and Public Service has installed bus stops for the No. 46 bus from Carteret to Perth Amboy and the No. 48 from Rahway to Perth Amboy. And for all to see, the sign atop the policeman's box (center left) proudly announces: "This is Woodbridge." (Bernie Anderson Jr.)

LOWER MAIN STREET, *c.* 1910. It is hard to imagine a time when children played ball in the middle of the business district! The Hungarian Reformed Church built in 1907 is visible on the left. Three years earlier the congregation named Reverend Alexander Vajo from Hungary as pastor, purchased five lots on School Street for $1,500 to build a church, and started a campaign to finance its construction.

SNOW DAY ON MAIN, *c.* 1910. Looks like snowplowing was kept to a minimum back then! Christensen's first store is visible on the far left. In 1895 Chris Christensen and his brother John Peter, from Denmark, founded Christensen's Department Store. This popular emporium made uniforms for the local police, and according to a 1924 advertisement, it sold "reliable clothing, men's furnishings, dry goods and shoes." The Methodist Church stands on the right. A few years later the steeple collapsed and was never replaced.

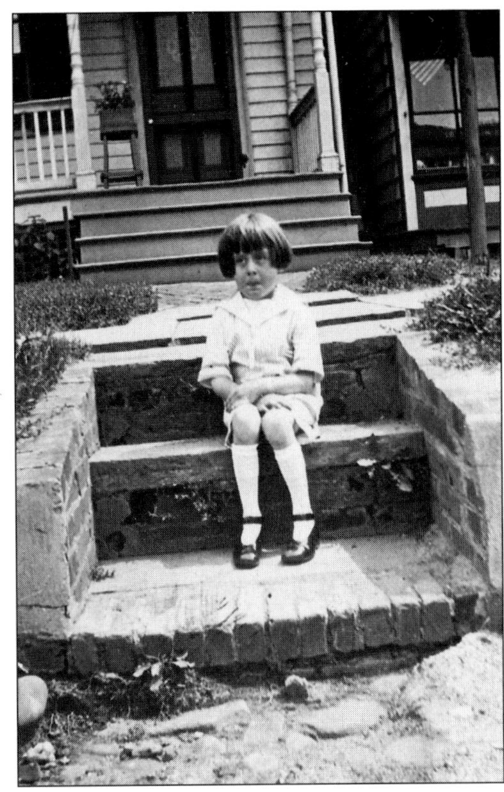

GEORGE PALMER STRICKER, *c.* 1920. Woodbridge's own "Buster Brown" sits on a neighbor's front steps next to John J. Neary's Butcher Shop (on right), which sold "Prime Meats Only." George's father, Matthew Stricker, owned a building across the street at 98 Main Street. Those were the days when little boys must have been continually warned by their anxious mothers not to wrinkle their clothes, scuff their shiny leather shoes, or dirty their spotless knee stockings. (Raymond Stricker)

NEW STORES ARRIVE, *c.* 1940. The first supermarket in town, the Acme (out of the picture), opened to the right of Dr. Herbert L. Moss's optometry office and introduced Woodbridge to the wonders of the shopping cart. An A&P Super Market and Woolworth's five and dime quickly followed to the left of Dr. Moss. A few years earlier Christensen's Department Store moved from across the street to 97 Main Street, a few doors to the left of Woolworth's. And note the advent of angle parking!

JACKSON'S CORNER, *c.* 1945. By this time the intersection of Main and School Streets was synonymous with Jackson and Son's Drug Store. During business hours a policeman kept traffic moving at this busy site; here Patrolman Horace Deter takes charge. High school students gathered on the corner (or hung out, if you will!) after school, stopping inside Jackson's for refreshments or simply to chat with the soda jerks who were officially called "fountaineers."

VETERANS' DRUM CORPS, *c.* 1900. Assembled in front of Blum's Grocery Store, the Woodbridge Sons of Veterans' Drum Corps and Firing Squad practice for a Memorial Day parade. Blum's was located where Pete Vogel would later open his liquor store and is now the location of Smiley's Country Deli and Gervin's Sport Shop. Identified veterans are, from left to right: (front row) Adam Gardner, Mr. Clark (third from left), Jacob Gardner with drum, Frank Gardner, John F. Gardner; (back row) Captain Inslee (fifth from left).

CORNER OF MAIN AND WILLIAM, *c.* 1910. In 1915 Morris and Lena Choper opened their department store here, a business which flourished for over fifty years. Mr. Choper spoke Polish when he came to town but soon learned Hungarian since many of his customers had come from Hungary to work in the nearby clay mines and brick factories.

THE NOE FAMILY, *c.* 1898. Gathered at the rear of the Central Hotel in the Phillips' Building (next door to Choper's) are, from left to right, Maidie, Aunt Mary, Etta, Lena Phillips Noe holding Eugene, Miles C. Noe, Raymond (with dog), and Sydney. In an advertisement for the hotel in the January 20, 1898 issue of *The Independent Hour*, Mr. Noe is listed as the proprietor. Other information included: "Board by the day, week or month. All orders by mail will receive prompt attention." (Rev. Philip Noe Nelson)

NEW GOVERNOR COMES TO TOWN, JULY 1913. On March 1, 1913, James F. Fiedler, president of the state senate, was appointed acting New Jersey governor, succeeding Woodrow Wilson who had been elected the twenty-eighth United States President. While visiting Woodbridge, Governor Fiedler (third man from left) and his entourage stepped out of their touring car in front of the First National Bank. Mr. Fiedler was elected governor in his own right later that year and served one term. (Pauline O'Connor)

THE CIRCUS COMES TO TOWN, *c.* 1924. Elephants parade on Main Street near William Street to announce the arrival of the circus. Across America traveling carnivals and circuses were an integral part of town life. Parades and posters summoned all to the "Big Top" usually set up in an outlying field. Because residents and businesses protested, such circuses and carnivals were banned in Woodbridge in 1928, but the resolution was often overlooked.

CARPENTER'S LIVERY STABLE, *c.* 1915. Located right off Main on Pearl Street, the stable housed the two well-known horse teams which pulled the first Woodbridge Fire Company hook and ladder wagon. "Tom" and "Harry" comprised the first team, "Buddie" and "Buster" the second. Blacksmith Larry Campion (center front) poses with stable personnel and horses. A few years later a devastating fire killed the horses and destroyed the stable even though townsmen quickly organized a bucket brigade and valiantly fought the blaze.

HORSE AND BUGGY, *c.* 1915. One of the beloved symbols of times past was the horse and carriage, which recalls the gentle "clippity-clop" of hooves, Sunday rides in the country, and a slower pace of life. Here a horse from Carpenter's Stable patiently awaits its driver on Main Street. One of the earliest "school buses" in town, a horse and wagon from Carpenter's, transported students from Port Reading and Carteret to School One with local resident Frederick A. Nelson at the reins. (Catherine Clark Burns)

THE 255TH ANNIVERSARY AND DEDICATION CELEBRATION, JUNE 14, 1924. A record-breaking crowd celebrated the Township anniversary and dedication of the Memorial Municipal Building at the east end of Main Street. The building (not visible here) stood to the right of the reviewing stand. According to a 96-page "Official Book" published for the occasion, the gala events of the day included a parade, dedication ceremonies at the platform (at right), inspection of the building, field events, competitions by neighboring firemen in "laying and reeling firehose and placing ladders," a block dance, and fireworks. Alfred J. Geiling of Fords designed a souvenir commemorative medal for the occasion which today is a collector's item. After World War I, Township citizens wanted to honor their servicemen with an appropriate memorial "as testimony of the municipality's gratitude. It was felt that this memorial should be of an utilitarian nature and, inasmuch as one of the great needs of the township had for many years been a larger and better appointed municipal building, it was decided to erect such a structure and dedicate it to the memory of the town's hero dead." The excavation for the new State Movie Theater partially circled by parked cars is visible on the left. (Madeline LaPenta Peterson)

LOCAL LANDMARK, 1924. Standing proudly at the foot of Main Street and serving for many years as center of the Township government, the Memorial Municipal Building represented the heart of Woodbridge for a long time. Despite citizens' protests, it was demolished in 1994 to make way for a large contemporary municipal building and parking garage.

SOLDIERS' AND SAILORS' MONUMENT, MAY 30, 1916. Plans for this statue began in 1910 when the local Kingwood Athletic Association initiated fund-raising activities to erect a monument at the east end of Main Street. Six years later residents dedicated this statue, which is inscribed, "In memory of the Soldiers and Sailors of Woodbridge, N. J., who fought in the wars of our Country." The statue still proudly stands at the spot where Main Street meets Rahway Avenue, reminding Woodbridge Township of the courage and sacrifice of its servicemen and women.

THE TOWN TURNS OUT, SUNDAY, OCTOBER 29, 1946. Some thirty thousand well-wishers lined local streets to officially welcome home the veterans of World War II. More than four thousand people took part in the Homecoming Parade led by Okinawa hero General George K. Nold; the Township Selective Service Board, Walter Warr, Hampton Cutter, and James J. Crowley; and parade chairman Charles E. Gregory, managing editor and publisher of *The Independent-Leader*. Vintage Reo Diner stands on the right.

HOMECOMING PARADE, OCTOBER 29, 1946. The Knights of Columbus march up Main Street past the Drake house, now the site of the Woodbridge Post Office. On Mother's Day in 1944, the honor roll plaque listing the names of all servicemen and women was dedicated on School Street in Woodbridge Park. Mrs. Harry Stankiewicz dedicated the plaque. She was the mother of U.S. Marine Robert J. Madden, first man from the town of Woodbridge killed in action during World War II.

Two

"Clay Was the Business of Our Township"

CLAY WAGON, *c.* 1890. Horses and men worked the Woodbridge clay pits. A single horse pulled a two-wheeled cart to move clay to nearby stockpiles, but for longer hauls to the factories and railroads a team of horses drew a four-wheeled wagon often traveling along Main Street. Pitmen using curved spades dug clay one lump at a time. If the pit became too deep for a man to toss the clay into a wagon, a horse-operated derrick lifted it out in a bucket. Four blacksmith shops put shoes on the one hundred and fifty horses who worked in the clay banks. They also made wagon repairs, and sharpened spades and hoes. A veterinarian remained on call day or night to tend to the horses' injuries and illnesses. (Middlesex Water Company)

SALAMANDER WORKS, *c.* 1880. One of the earliest brick factories, possibly the first in New Jersey, opened in Woodbridge in 1825. French immigrants Michael Lefoulon and Henry De Casse founded the Salamander Works at Main Street and Rahway Avenue and built it into a successful company manufacturing cupola linings, firebricks, furnace blocks, slabs, bakers' ovens, and greenhouse tile, as well as sewer, drain, and heating pipes. William Poillon of New York City purchased the company in 1867 and three years later expanded it to include pottery making. By 1882 the company employed one hundred and twenty-five people and maintained eight fire kilns which were heated day and night. Relatives of Mr. Poillon, Clara Louise Poillon, and Mrs. Howard A. Poillon founded the C.L. and H.A. Poillon Pottery Company in 1901 in Jersey City to manufacture artware. They later moved the company to Woodbridge. Poillon earthenware was decorated in flat and high-gloss glazes of green, yellow, blue, and other colors. The women displayed their specialty artware at New York City ceramic exhibitions in the early 1900s.

SALAMANDER EMPLOYEES, *c.* 1900. By looking closely at the workers' clothes and shoes, it's possible to guess what each man did for a living. Suits and watch chains would indicate office workers, while dusty shoes and aprons indicate those working with the bricks. The origin of the unusual name "Salamander" is unknown. Perhaps the founders named their company for the salamander or lizard of Egyptian and French mythology which could withstand searing heat. Or maybe there were salamanders in Heard's Brook that ran through the company property! (Kathy Jost Keating)

HENRY MAURER, *c.* 1857. Henry Maurer, a cabinetmaker from Germany, purchased the Excelsior Fire Brick and Clay Retort Works about 1874 from Charles Anness and Son. At that time the company included 75 acres close to the Woodbridge border in what has become known as the Maurer section of Perth Amboy. Mr. Maurer also owned 11 acres of clay banks in Woodbridge and a mile of waterfront along the Woodbridge River. His tiles were used on the roof of the New Jersey Building at the Philadelphia Centennial in 1876.

WILLIAM H. BERRY, *c.* 1850. A native of Maine, Mr. Berry operated a firm in Jersey City involved in the baling and shipping of hay before he settled in Woodbridge in 1832. He is credited with introducing the sale of clean burning, anthracite coal to the Township. In 1845 he opened his successful firebrick manufacturing plant at the foot of Berry Street. During the Civil War, Mr. Berry's son, William C. Berry, served as a first lieutenant with the Fifth New Jersey Volunteers and was killed in the Battle of Williamsburg in 1862. He was the first Woodbridge citizen killed in the Civil War and the GAR Post No. 85 was named in his honor.

HAMPTON CUTTER, *c.* 1850. Mr. Cutter (1811–1882), farmer and clay merchant, descended from a Massachusetts family who settled in Woodbridge in 1706. In 1845 Mr. Cutter made a fortuitous discovery on his property in the Strawberry Hill section. He struck a large deposit of kaolin, a fine white clay used in the manufacture of porcelain. Five years later he founded Hampton Cutter and Son, a company which mined kaolin, other fire clays, and sand. On January 26, 1836, Mr. Cutter married Mary R. Crane of Cranford, New Jersey.

JOSIAH C. (LEFT) AND WILLIAM H. CUTTER, *c.* 1870. Josiah (1836–1871), the oldest son of Hampton and Mary Crane Cutter, was associated with his father in the clay business. He also served as an officer of the Woodbridge Dime Savings Bank until his untimely death. Hampton Cutter's younger son William (1840–1918) married Sarah R., daughter of local resident Samuel Barron, in 1871. He took over the clay mining business when his father died in 1882. Their two children, Hampton and Laura, lived in Woodbridge all their lives.

WILLIAM H. CUTTER'S WEST CLAY BANKS, *c.* 1890. A blessing from nature, Woodbridge clay in the form of granular mineral deposits arrived here through the action of glaciers, rivers, and streams. These minerals settled out in the layers which provide clay for various products. In March 1930, newspapers carried the astonishing story that workers at the Cutter Clay Banks had uncovered four dinosaur footprints, each measuring about 20 inches in length. When Roy E. Anderson, manager of operations, announced this find, scientists from Yale and Rutgers Universities and the Museum of Natural History rushed to the site. The footprints were carefully extracted and sent to Rutgers where casts were made for museums.

M.D. VALENTINE AND BRO., *c.* 1875. This well-known manufacturer of firebricks, glazed drain pipe, land tile, sewer pipe, and refractory shapes was founded in 1866 by brothers Mulford D. and James Valentine. Other early Woodbridge clay and brick companies included: Mutton Hollow Fire Brick Co., Anness and Potter Fire Clay Co., Ostrander Brick Works, National Fireproofing Company and General Ceramics in Keasbey, Atlantic Terra Cotta Co., McHose Clay Co., Melick Bros. Clay Mining Co., and C.W. Boynton's Drain Pipe and Tile Works.

M.D. VALENTINE CO., 1939. For many years Valentine's firebricks were considered the best in the world. Woodbridge clay, classified as a sedimentary clay, was in demand for many applications, especially in the steel and ceramic fields because it could tolerate extremely high temperatures. In 1901 New Jersey produced the largest amount of clay in the United States. The Valentine factory was located at the southern end of Fulton Street on the east side of the N.J. Transit railroad tracks. (Andrew Csepcsar)

VALENTINE BRICK HAULING TRUCK, *c.* 1925. No soft ride for the bricks in this truck! Just look at those solid rubber tires—tires that never had a flat! Since shipping was always a vital link in the manufacturing process of clay products, Valentine's established a branch factory in 1887 along the Lehigh Valley Railroad on Upper Main Street. The company also maintained a railroad siding at their main plant for transporting goods on the Pennsylvania Railroad. (Andrew Csepcsar)

M.D. VALENTINE FIRE, 1956. After the entire factory was consumed by a devastating fire, it was rebuilt with modern equipment and within eleven months was operating again. During this time all employees were kept on the payroll. Two years later it became a division of the A.P. Green Fire Brick Company of Mexico, Missouri, until 1985, when Valentine's ceased production. One fire kiln remains on the property today, reminding Woodbridge residents of a once proud and highly productive native industry. (Andrew Csepcsar)

GEORGE DUNHAM HOUSE, *c.* 1924. This once recognizable homestead near Mutton Hollow Drive is shown here at the time of the realignment of Upper Main Street through the clay banks. Previously Main Street had circled around the clay area as the road continued into Fords and on into New Brunswick. In a 1902 membership directory of the Woodbridge Methodist Church, Mrs. George Dunham's address is listed as "Beyond Clay Banks." (Ray Schneider)

WOODBRIDGE RIVER DOCK, MAY 9, 1935. Anness Hollow Tile plant superintendent Frank Boka (left) supervises the loading of clay onto a schooner for shipment to Taunton, Massachusetts, for use in the manufacturing of pottery. The ship captain was F. Slade Dole from Bay Head, New Jersey. (Frank Boka)

FOREST L. SIMMONS, 1935. Three times a year 500 tons of raw clay from the Anness Hollow Tile Company were loaded aboard this wide-beam schooner anchored at the Woodbridge River Dock. These shipments by water ceased at the end of that year. Early in the 1920s the demand for Woodbridge clay began a rapid decline. New continuous "car kilns" replaced the old "periodic" kilns. In the old kilns each article was placed in a clay container for protection from the fire soot. Now these containers were no longer needed. A greater factor in the downturn for New Jersey clays involved the development of new clay beds in Tennessee, Kentucky, Georgia, the Carolinas, Pennsylvania, Ohio, Florida, and other states. New Jersey could not match the lower transportation rates available elsewhere. (Frank Boka)

ANNESS CO-WORKERS, *c.* 1935. Plant superintendent Frank Boka (left) and co-workers pose with some of their company's clay products, such as hollow tile. In his article "Woodbridge and its Clays," the late John Kreger, Township ceramic consultant, stated, "Our town must have been greatly dependent on the clay industry, both in the actual mining, shipping and the subsequent processing into ceramic commodities. Clay was the business of our Township. Never again will Woodbridge be blessed with a single industry that employed such a large percentage of its population as did clay." (Frank Boka)

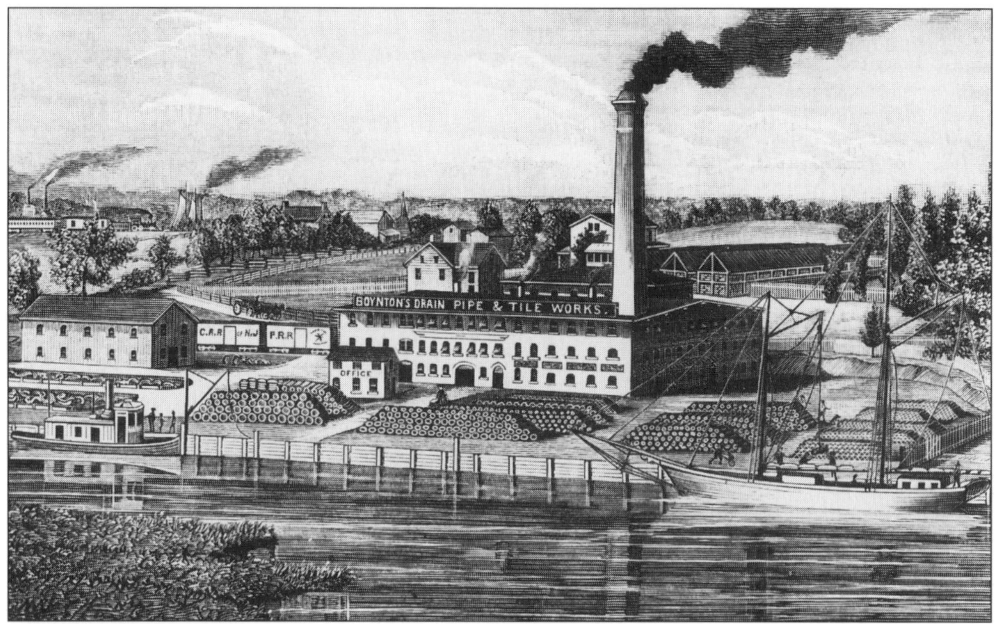

C.W. BOYNTON'S DRAIN PIPE AND TILE WORKS, 1882. This woodcut says it all by tracing the clay industry from mining to shipping. Horses and wagons haul the clay to the factory. A worker moves the finished product to storage piles, and boxcars and a schooner wait for loading. John Kreger closes his article on clay by saying, "It would be fitting for our Town Fathers to erect somewhere in this area . . . a monument in testimony and acknowledgment to Clay for all that it has meant to the Township of Woodbridge in its early, formative years."

Three

School Days, School Days

WOODBRIDGE ACADEMY, *c.* 1844. A very early school, Woodbridge Academy, is located in the left foreground of this wood engraving. The Barron house is located on the far right with the Presbyterian Church at center right and the Trinity Episcopal Church next to it in the distance. Built in 1793, the Academy opened as a semi-private school where students were charged to attend. Eliza Fitz Randolph paid $125 tuition in 1826. By 1870 all Woodbridge Township schools were free.

SCHOOL ONE, *c.* 1890. A beloved Woodbridge landmark, forever called School One, was built in 1876 with twelve classrooms for grades one through eleven. (In 1897 the high school curriculum was expanded to four years.) School One was the first school in the Township to have separate classes for each grade. When it opened, Harry Anderson was appointed principal at a salary of $100 a month; Sarah E. Eldridge, vice principal at $600 for 11 months; and Kate A. Moore, teacher at $400 for 11 months. The trustees (an early name for Board of Education members) purchased a clock and a 1,500 lb. bell for the tower. The bell was inscribed "School District #24, A.D. 1876. C.W. Boynton, President: Howard Valentine, D.C. (District Clerk), William H. Berry and Charles Campbell, Trustees. Wisdom is better than gold." At the dedication exercises for the school, Mr. Berry announced that the building and land had cost $25,000 and that $2,300 more was needed to finish. This old sturdy building continues in use today as the administration offices for the Township schools.

WOODBRIDGE ACADEMY TRIPLE DESK, *c.* 1793. Imagine sitting on a hard, backless bench close to two other students and trying to study! In such cramped quarters whispering, poking elbows, and, yes, copying would have been quite easy. Of course, in those early times harried teachers might use dunce caps and hickory sticks to maintain an orderly classroom. Board of Education records show that in 1843 a female teacher was relieved of her duties at the Academy because she was a poor disciplinarian.

SCHOOL STREET SCENE, *c.* 1908. The newly constructed Hungarian Reformed Church in the left foreground and an enlarged School One next door are clear evidence that Woodbridge was a growing community. By 1909 this school was so overcrowded that classes were held in the Hungarian Parish House and across School Street in the firehouse.

Rules for Teachers 1872

1. *Teachers each day will fill lamps, trim the wicks and clean chimneys.*

2. *Each morning teacher will bring a bucket of water and a scuttle of coal for the day's session.*

3. *Make your pens carefully. You may whittle nibs to the individual taste of the pupils.*

4. *Men teachers may take one evening each week for courting purposes, or two evenings a week if they attend church regularly.*

5. *After ten hours in school, the teachers may spend the remaining time reading the Bible or any other good books.*

6. *Women teachers who marry or engage in unseemly conduct will be dismissed.*

7. *Every teacher should lay aside from each pay a goodly sum of his earnings for his benefit during his declining years so that he will not become a burden on society.*

8. *Any teacher who smokes, uses liquor in any form, frequents pool or public halls, or gets shaved in a barber shop will give good reason to suspect his worth, intention, integrity and honesty.*

9. *The teacher who performs his labor faithfully and without fault for five years will be given an increase of twenty-five cents per week in his pay, providing the Board of Education approves.*

COMMANDMENTS FOR TEACHERS, NINETEENTH-CENTURY STYLE. No doubt about it, a teacher's day didn't end when the last school bell rang!

TYPICAL CLASSROOM, *c.* 1895. Not a smile or a silly grin can be detected among these third- or fourth-grade youngsters seated in their School One classroom. In these early days the classrooms were lighted with kerosene lamps tended by the teacher (a lamp is visible on upper left side of the room).

MISS MAE KELLY'S FOURTH OR FIFTH GRADERS, 1896. Some of the students pictured here at School One are Fanny Deter, Emma Hendrickson, Charles Sorensen, Earl Valentine, Joseph McEwen, Walter Zeltemeyer, Robert Fullerton, Kate Miller, Rachel Moore, Fred Nelson, Eugene Romand, John Ramberg, Joe Zehrer, Charles Einhorn, Austin Anderson, Charles Nelson, Albert Sadler, Alfred Mundy, and Albert Simonsen.

CLASS OF 1888. With their Principal A.H. Wilson (far left), Woodbridge High School graduates (standing from left) Margaret Miller, Arthur Valentine, Paul R. Lewis, Gorham Boynton; (seated) Lillian N. Browning, Adeline S. Anness, and Willard P. Melick appear ready to face the world. The first recorded high school class graduated in 1883 with two students.

JOHN H. LOVE, *c.* 1920. Dr. Love came to town in 1895 to serve as teaching principal of Woodbridge High School. In 1900 he was named the first supervising principal of the Township schools. (Later the title was changed to superintendent.) Dr. Love was also one of the first in town to own an automobile. By the time he retired in June 1933, each section of the Township had its own elementary school, designated by a number which replaced such colorful school names as Mt. Pleasant, Blazing Star, Locust Grove, Rahway Neck, and Six Roads.

EIGHTH-GRADE GRADUATES, 1907. Boutonnieres, bouquets, and corsages were certainly the order of the day at School One for the Township's eighth grade graduates. From left to right, the graduates are Thora Louise Thomsen, mother of Images of America: *Woodbridge* author Robert J. McEwen; Roger Gimbernat; Helen Valentine; Theresa Fowler; Alice Turner; Ruth Valentine; Thomas Cody; Edna Weber; Annie Lunt; Verna Love; Susie Farren; Charles Campbell; Josephine McGowan; Ruth Gilman; teacher Miss Fownes; John Kuhn; Annie Rohde; and Edward Weber.

WOODBRIDGE HIGH SCHOOL ORCHESTRA, 1907. Students ready to make music are, from left to right: (front row) William Gardner and Clarence Gillis; (second row) Anna Waring, teacher Miss E. Cornish, and Charles A. Treen; (third row) William Prall and Asher Fitz Randolph; (standing in back) William DeHaven, Clarence Olsen, and Alfred Johnson. Supervising Principal John H. Love played the flute and often joined the orchestra rehearsals.

HIGH SCHOOL CORNERSTONE DEDICATION, OCTOBER 6, 1910. New Jersey Governor J. Franklin Fort laid the cornerstone for Woodbridge High School, which opened the following year and remained the only Township high school until 1956. As part of the festivities, Woodbridge schoolchildren waving flags paraded down Green Street to Barron Avenue to join in this dedication which marked the official first step toward a much needed high school.

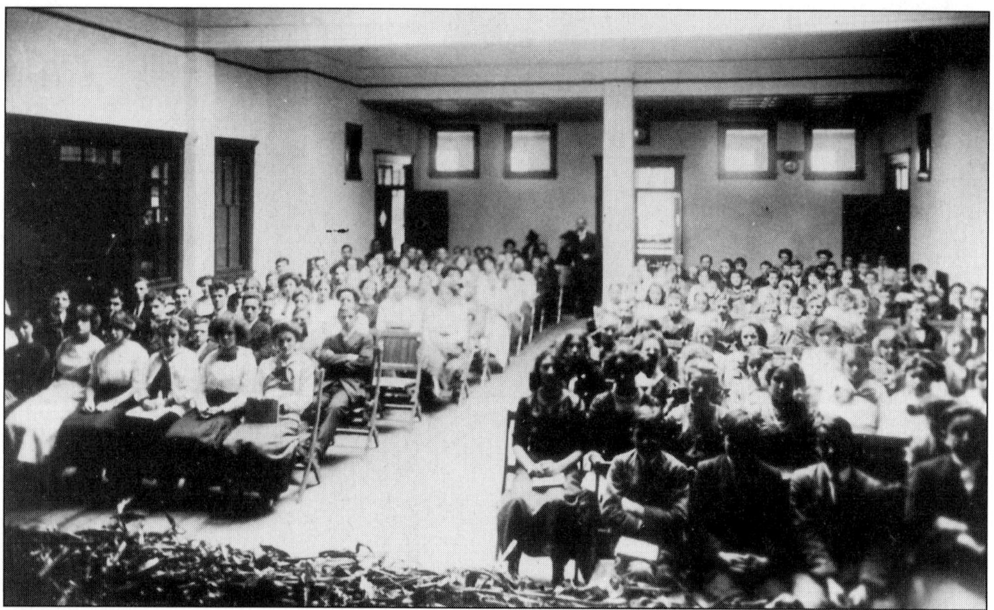

WHS ASSEMBLY ROOM, 1911. Cornstalks decorated the assembly room at the newly finished Woodbridge High School. Until a new wing was added to the school in 1925, students gathered in this room for programs and morning exercises. The addition contained an auditorium, chemistry lab, gymnasium, physical training room, and cafeteria.

WHS STUDY HALL, 1911. Another early photo shows high school pupils catching up on their homework. Students followed a dress code in this era, whether mandated by the administration or simply understood by all. No boy would have arrived without a jacket and tie, and no girl would have dared wear anything but a long skirt and middy blouse or a proper dress. And those taking physical training would have discreetly carried their sneakers and gymsuits in a suitable bag.

"OUR BACKFIELD GOES ROLLING ALONG," 1915. An early football team faces the camera in front of the new Woodbridge High School. For many years this familiar building was the alma mater for all Township high school graduates. In September 1933, the school started operating on a double session to accommodate the huge rise in enrollment. Freshmen attended in the afternoon, upperclass students in the morning. The double session continued until 1964, several years after the new high school opened on Kelly Street.

The Class of Nineteen Eleven

Woodbridge High School

requests your presence at the

Commencement Exercises

to be held in the

Presbyterian Church

Friday Evening, June the sixteenth

at eight o'clock

Class of Nineteen Eleven

Class Motto: Verbesserung

Class Colors: Green and Gold

Graduates

Classical Course

E. John Kuhn

Ruth Valentine

Modern Language Course

Verna Delmar Love

Commercial Course

Josephine Lawrence McGowan

Thora Louise Thomsen

WOODBRIDGE HIGH SCHOOL COMMENCEMENT INVITATION, 1911. Since the high school had no auditorium, commencement exercises were held at the First Presbyterian Church until the mid-1920s.

WHS BAND, APRIL 3, 1941. Always a source of pride in their smart red and black jackets and white pants, the Woodbridge High School band was an all-male group of instrumentalists at this time. High school principal Arthur Ferry stands on the left and band director Theodore H. Hoops at the far right.

FIRST DAY OF SCHOOL, 1915. High button shoes and hair bows identified these young scholars reporting to School One on opening day. From left to right, the students are: (front row) Blanche Huber, Ida Weber, Cynthia Ware, Eva Whalen, Marie Bobzine, Grace Chapik, Helen Dockstader, Irene Posse, Olga Formidoni, Margaret Voorhees, and unidentified child (photo damaged); (second row) Ella LaPenta, Mary Zeto, Anna Galowbuski, Margaret Toth, Harold Ringwood, Frank Nagy, John Palko, Rudolph Durish, and Donald Noe; (third row) Stevie Sisco, Albert Hegedus, Valentine Brown, Clifford Jaeger, George Hausman, Martin Snyder, Stanley Knapek, and Andrew Orlick; (top row) teacher Sophie Johnson, unidentified child, Willie Schlectmeyer, Victor Hall, Joseph Bartone, Charles Luffbary, John Kosa, unidentified child, and Alec Tellesick.

FACULTY OF SCHOOL 11, *c.* 1934. Teachers are, from left to right: (front row) Elsie Agreen, Sadie Whitaker, Elizabeth Kopper, Jane Dunigan, Mary Mack Gagdosh, Sylvia Mucciarello, Gladys Sitzer, and Clara Skidmore; (second row) Arlene Corlute, Adrian DeYoung, unidentified, Helen Mullin, Carlotta Mason, and unidentified; (third row) Ruth Tracy, Jean Johnson, Ethel Inslee, Anna C. Fraser; (fourth row) Helen Coan, Effie K. Neville, Amelia List Schrimpf, unidentified, and Alice Finn Lowassy; (top row) Harold B. Goetschius, Roland Lund, Nellie Edgar, Margaret Henricksen, and Leonard Willinger.

BOARD OF EDUCATION, 1924. The trustees of the Woodbridge Township schools always faced tough financial, logistical, and educational decisions in dealing with their rapidly growing system. Shown here from left to right are: (seated) Maurice Dunigan, Mrs. Harry J. Baker, President Melvin H. Clum, Mrs. Albert L. Gardner, and Board Clerk Everett C. Ensign; (standing) Roy E. Anderson, three unidentified members, and Supervising Principal John H. Love.

FREE SCHOOL LANDS MAP, c. 1964. When Governor Philip Carteret chartered Woodbridge in 1669, he deeded property to the settlers to support a free school system. These colonists from Massachusetts greatly valued education and wanted funds set aside for their children's learning. The tract contained about 160 acres and became known as the Free School Lands. Through the centuries, attempts were made to sell the land, but it wasn't until the 1960s that a legal sale was finally arranged.

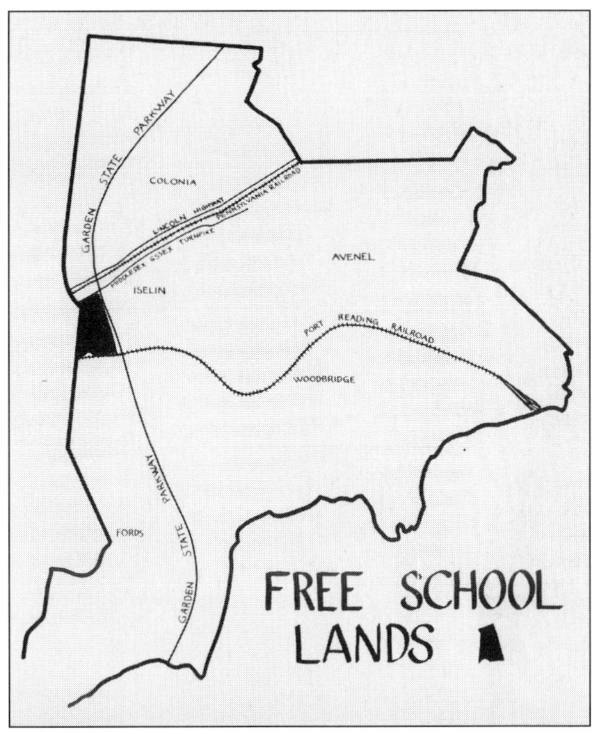

FREE SCHOOL LANDS TRUSTEES, 1924. For years the elected trustees were all gentlemen. Later when ladies became the only candidates for the three-year posts, they were called "The Seven Sisters." This picture included in the *Municipal Building Dedication Booklet* shows President Marguerite Fitz Randolph seated at center. Other members not identified in order are M. Frances McCarter, Catherine D. Flanagan, Martha Ernst, Helen M. DeRussy, Helen Pfeiffer, and Grace Von Bremen.

UNIONTOWN SCHOOL, ISELIN, *c.* 1890. A reporter for the local newspaper, *Independent Hour*, published this entertaining account of a visit to the school on June 14, 1877, for a combined spelling bee, oral geography test, and special exhibition of Alexander Graham Bell's telephone using Thomas Edison's carbon button. It was perhaps the first public demonstration in the country of the carbon button, a device which greatly improved the mechanism into which one speaks. Edison's workshops at Menlo Park were located near the school. "Many who attended the exhibition were agreeably surprised to find that Mr. Edison of Menlo Park had placed his telephone in the house for the entertainment of the visitors. The felicity of hearing as well as seeing so recent and wonderful an invention could not fail to make it unusually impressive, especially to all interested in progress and enlightenment and although all the instruments and connections were only temporarily arranged and the operators not all practiced yet the result was most gratifying. Only the least amount of testing and we had selections from Mr. Sankey's hymns as well as National Airs—My Country 'Tis of Thee—being transmitted with wonderful clearness. We should not be at all surprised if Edison taught this child of inventive fancy to talk," (Signed) "Progress."

FIRE HOUSE SCHOOL, AVENEL, *c.* 1910. The Avenel section of the Township temporarily solved two community challenges by opening an elementary school on the second floor of this building and a firehouse on the first. The central double doors must have been wide enough to accommodate the firefighting equipment. The teacher at this time was Miss O. Harvey.

WASHINGTON SCHOOL, AVENEL, *c.* 1920. Known originally as the Six Roads School, this early school house was located on King George's Road (later St. George Avenue). It was one of thirteen free public schools in operation in the Township by 1869. Like other early schools, Washington School outlived its usefulness and was replaced by the Avenel School. The building was sold for $75 and later demolished.

TYPICAL TOWNSHIP SCHOOLS, *c.* 1924. The 1920s and early 1930s were a time of continued school growth and construction. In 1926 the elementary schools of the Township were divided into two sections: Keasbey, Fords, and Hopelawn schools were named the South Side schools, while the remaining Woodbridge Township schools became known as the North Side.

Four
Sewaren

"ROW, ROW, ROW YOUR BOAT," 1916. Since many people worked six days a week, this outing on the waters of the Arthur Kill was probably on a Sunday. Both gentlemen appear relaxed at their oars, but the ladies may be holding their breath lest a shift of weight or wind topple them all overboard. Just think of those beautiful hats floating away and the struggle to swim in long dresses! Boat eleven may have been rented from Acker's Grove or from the Boynton Beach boat house, both popular spots on the Sewaren waterfront.

BOYNTON BEACH SIGNED PRINT, *c.* 1980. New Jersey artist Anna Gross painted this limited edition watercolor for the Historical Association of Woodbridge Township to sell as a fund-raiser. The artist used vintage postcards of Boynton Beach as models. C.W. Boynton, a local manufacturer of brick and sewer pipe as well as an astute businessman, saw resort possibilities in Sewaren and opened Boynton Beach in 1877. His resort complex included a bathing beach, bathhouses, a dance pavilion, pony rides, a shooting gallery, nickelodeon, a

bowling alley, amusement rides, a restaurant featuring New York City chefs, and a fleet of one hundred rowboats. By decree of Mr. Boynton, a teetotaler, the resort was free of alcoholic beverages. Boynton Beach was the "place to be" for many years but later declined in popularity when the automobile provided vacationers with more distant options. The name Boynton Beach, however, lives on in Florida where a resort town was named for Sewaren's favored vacation spot.

BOYNTON BEACH ATTRACTIONS, *c.* 1910. Two symbols long associated with summer fun, the hot dog stand and the merry-go-round (on right), operated side by side at Boynton Beach, also called Sewaren Beach. Although most folks traveled to the resort by ferry, trolley, train, and bicycle, some began arriving in automobiles.

BOYNTON BEACH DANCING PAVILION, *c.* 1910. C.W. Boynton's hardwood dance floor quickly gained a reputation as one of the best in the state. Mr. Boynton hired orchestras to play for the gala dances held every Saturday evening all summer. Whether dancing inside or outside the pavilion, young and old alike wore their finest clothes. Boynton Beach was a special place where visitors put their "best foot forward."

FERRIS WHEEL, *c.* 1907. Towering high over the Boynton Beach landscape, this exhilarating ride, originally known as the pleasure wheel, surely attracted a lively following. George W. Gale Ferris, a mechanical engineer from Galesburg, Illinois, built the largest wheel ever for the Columbian Exposition in 1893, thereby attaching his name to the now familiar amusement ride.

THE BAMBOO SLIDE, *c.*1900. In a rare moment these well-dressed youngsters stop short amid their downward slide to have their picture snapped. This curious, curving slide must have provided many screams and squeals of laughter for young Boynton Beach vacationers.

BOYNTON BEACH

COLORED SALT WATER DAY

WEDNESDAY JULY 23d

Bathing -- Boating -- Dancing

ALL ATTRACTIONS

Come And Bring The Children.

"SALT WATER DAY FOR COLORED PEOPLE," *c*. 1913. Until after World War II many resort areas were segregated or allowed only white people to come. Boynton Beach was no different except for one July day each year when the management invited African Americans to enjoy the resort. (Catherine Clark Burns)

"ORANGEADE TOUCHES THE SPOT," 1906. Come and get your ice cream sodas, orangeade, and phosphates! Long gone from the soft drink scene, phosphates were sparkling beverages made from carbonated water and a dash of phosphoric acid flavored with lemon or other fruit syrup.

ON BOYNTON BEACH, *c.* 1912. Woodbridge resident Etta Noe (left) and friends enjoy a day on the sands of Boynton Beach. It's hard to determine whether the girls' fashionable frocks are for bathing in the Arthur Kill or simply to shade them from the sun. Etta Noe later married Frederick Axel Nelson. The couple raised their sons, Frederick, Louis, and Philip on St. George Avenue, Woodbridge. (Rev. Philip Noe Nelson)

EXCURSIONISTS ARRIVING BY WATER, *c.* 1900. In 1892 C.W. Boynton purchased the steamboat "Pauline" to run every Tuesday and Saturday from Sewaren to Bayonne and Elizabethport. Later a steamboat sailing daily between New Brunswick and New York City stopped at the Sewaren House Hotel to deliver mail and passengers and take on locally grown salt hay for the New York market. Mr. Boynton and other area businessmen knew that accessible transportation was their key to a profitable and popular resort.

THE SEWAREN HOUSE HOTEL, *c.* 1895. In its golden days this summer hotel was crowded with vacationers from New Jersey and New York who came to enjoy the salt air and sparkling water of the Arthur Kill. (The Dutch word "kill" meaning creek or river dates back to the early seventeenth century when the area was under Dutch control.) Hotel guests, who included Thomas Alva Edison and the actress Maude Adams, often gathered on the spacious veranda (photo at center right) to catch the sea breezes as well as the latest happenings on the summer

circuit. Another famous guest, President Grover Cleveland, a New Jersey native, came to fish. Built in 1887 by Robert DeForest, the hotel was located south of Ferry Street on the beach side of Cliff Road. Mr. DeForest was the son-in-law of Robert Taylor Johnston, a developer of Sewaren and president of the Central Railroad of New Jersey. The Sewaren House Hotel closed its doors in 1913 and was demolished in 1923. The Shell Oil Company occupies most the site today with some of the land owned by the Royal Petroleum Division of Kerr-McGee.

ACKER'S GROVE AND BOATHOUSE, *c*. 1910. As well as operating his boathouse and picnic grove, Henry Acker, the first of his family to settle in Sewaren, raised plants for seeds which he sold to the Peter Henderson Seed Company. For several years the Ackers also owned a canning factory in Sewaren employing about forty women to process tomatoes grown in nearby fields. Their glass jars of tomatoes were prized commodities among local housewives. Another family member R.O. Acker built boats.

GO TO
ACKER'S
SEWAREN, N. J.

Bathing – Boating – Crabbing

SKEE BALL ALLEYS
and
OTHER AMUSEMENTS

AQUATIC MEETS AT FREQUENT INTERVALS

Easily reached by Newark Fast Line and Rahway Line cars

ACKER'S ADVERTISEMENT, JUNE 1924. Located next to the Sewaren House Hotel, Acker's attractions flourished for many years after the hotel and Boynton Beach closed. Eventually, the Acker property became part of the oil industry complex. This advertisement appeared in the program booklet distributed at the dedication of the Woodbridge Municipal Building.

THE LAND AND WATER CLUB, *c.* 1910. For years the social life of Sewaren residents revolved around this boating club organized in 1892. Article II of the Club Rules stated that the "objective of the Club shall be the mental and physical improvement of the members." Although primarily involved in yachting competitions, the club staged elegant dances where gentlemen dressed in full evening regalia, and ladies wore silk and satin ball gowns complete with long white kid gloves. Boating activities also took place at the Sewaren Motor Boat Club on Smith's Creek.

C.W. BALLARD HOUSE, *c.* 1895. One of Sewaren's influential families, the C.W. Ballards, made their home in this Queen Anne-style house on Cliff Road. Since it was built, the house has been owned by only three families. The Ballards sold the house, called "Cedar Cliff," to Charles Lewis. In 1927 Horatio D. Clark, executive secretary of the Toy Manufacturers' Association of America in New York City, purchased the house which has remained in the Clark/Burns family since that time.

WOODBRIDGE FERRY, 1890. This unique ferryboat transported passengers across the Woodbridge River from State Street, Perth Amboy to West Avenue, Sewaren. The boat had neither sails nor engine. With ferryman Eric Anderson at the helm, the boat was pulled from bank to bank by a chain which ran through the ferry over an idler pulley. The boat was a primitive conveyance consisting of a wooden platform built on a barge and covered with a flat roof. A picket fence surrounded its sides to keep passengers safely on board. Whatever its shortcomings, the fare of 2¢ each way seems quite reasonable by any standards. The demise of the ferry came in the early 1900s when a trolley bridge was built across the river. Before the ferry, two enterprising boys with a rowboat provided passenger service on an irregular schedule.

PUBLIC SERVICE TROLLEY BRIDGE, OCTOBER 25, 1910. C.W. Boynton was instrumental in extending the Rahway-Woodbridge Trolley to Sewaren in 1895 to provide reasonably priced transportation for daytrippers to reach Boynton Beach. When the bridge was built, it extended trolley service to Perth Amboy and provided access for individuals and horse transportation to cross the Woodbridge River. The sign "Walk Your Horses" (center of bridge) reminded horseback riders and carriage drivers to keep their horses safely under control while crossing the trolley bridge.

BOYNTON BEACH TROLLEY STATION, *c.* 1910. Year-round passengers to Woodbridge and Rahway found that hopping the Woodbridge and Sewaren Electric Street Railway Company trolley at the Sewaren turnaround provided an easy commute to work. The line later continued to Perth Amboy after the trolley bridge was built and remained in business until Public Service replaced it with bus service in the early 1930s.

CENTRAL RAILROAD STATION, SEWAREN, *c.* 1930. This picturesque building saw many vacationers pass through its doors. John Taylor Johnston, who also built the railroad stations in Matawan and Long Branch, gave annual prizes for the best maintained gardens and grounds around the stations. Since the community did not have mail delivery during the resort era, the station also served for a time as the post office. Townsfolk picked up their mail there, and summer guests purchased 1¢ stamps for the postcards they mailed to family and friends.

W.T. AMES BUILDING, *c.* 1924. Andrew Kath maintained his grocery and vegetable store in this building on the south side of Woodbridge Avenue near Meade Street. William T. Ames, owner of the building, served as president of the First National Bank of Woodbridge. For years small grocery, newspaper, and drug stores provided both needed commodities and the news of the day to neighborhood residents.

PROGRAM COVER, AMBULANCE FUND ENTERTAINMENT, JULY 20, 1918. Spearheaded by Nathan Robins Jr. and Frederick H. Turner, a committee of Sewaren residents sponsored an elaborate evening of entertainment to raise funds to purchase an ambulance for the American armed forces in France during World War I. The benefit was inspired by two Sewaren citizens: Sergeant Roger Gimbernat, a member of the Hospital Unit of the American Expeditionary Forces in France, and Ruth Ballard, who attended the benefit and later served in France with the Ambulance Service. The committee hoped that Roger might drive the ambulance provided by Sewaren once it reached France. The program booklet for the evening included poignant letters written home by local servicemen. (Catherine Clark Burns)

SEWAREN BABY BOOM, *c.* 1925. Whoever snapped this photo must have been patient indeed to have captured on film so many of Sewaren's younger generation! Mothers include, from left to right: (front row) Marie Giroud, Linda Ames (wearing hat with turned-up brim), Irene Wiswall, Isabel Rankin, and Florence S. Clark. Maxine MacCallum stands at far left. Others are unidentified. (Catherine Clark Burns)

CLIFF ROAD, *c.* 1950. Built as "summer cottages," these stately mansions are lasting reminders of Sewaren's days as a fashionable summer resort. The oil industry's huge tanks and encroaching presence may be visible in the distance, but Sewaren continues to this day as a vibrant, vital section of Woodbridge Township.

Five
Our Finest

MEMORIAL DAY, 1924. All but one of the twenty-four members of the Woodbridge Police Department are gathered here for a final photo at the first Town Hall located on School Street by Heard's Brook. Two weeks later, the Township business was moved to the new Municipal Building on Main Street. Built in 1883, the old Town Hall housed the courtroom, the police lock-up, and several meeting rooms. Pictured from left to right are: Benjamin Parsons, Carl Sunquist, George Keating, Joseph Einhorn, John Egan, Harvey Romond, Thomas Somers, Wilhelm Brown, James Walsh, Dan Gibson, Patrick Cullinane, Joseph Makfinsky, Patrick Murphy, Andy Simonsen, Philip Dunphy, August Matthews, Fred Larsen, John Cholar, Robert Egan, Edward Oldbrick, Hans Simonsen, George Balint, and Joe Lewis. (Bernie Anderson Sr.)

WOODBRIDGE'S FIRST POLICEMAN, 1910. Patrick Cullinane (left), shown here with future Welfare Director John Omenhiser, was appointed constable in 1895 and a police officer the following year. According to a local newspaper article written at the time of "Paddy's" death in 1937, he was a beloved, larger-than-life figure known for his generosity, physical strength, and hilarious stories. Officer Cullinane grew up on his family's farm on Metuchen Avenue. In his youth he strengthened his muscles digging clay and driving clay wagons. Apparently, the only times he really tested his legendary prowess were at the annual firemen's picnics at Washington Hall on Grove Street. During these affairs his tug-of-war team was pitted against Police Chief Patrick Murphy's team. Paddy against Paddy—"that was a sight to see. . . . Woodbridge was a much, much better place to live because of Patrick Cullinane. . . . Fearless, unconquerable, shrewd and clean . . . the man lived an epic life which is probably the reason that epics were constructed around his exploits while he was still adding to the list of them." (Dorothy Omenhiser McCabe)

DECORATION DAY PARADE, *c.* 1920. Woodbridge's first police chief, Patrick Murphy, takes the lead up Green Street past Pete Greiner's Barber Shop. Officer Murphy served as chief from 1911 to 1932. Unfortunately, Memorial Day parades are no longer held in Woodbridge, but for years these celebrations brought the community together to honor the patriotism, commitment, and sacrifice of earlier generations.

MOTORCYCLE SQUAD, MEMORIAL DAY, 1928. (From left to right) Benjamin Parsons, Carl Sundquist, George Balint, and Joe Lewis stop outside the Municipal Building. When this new Town Hall opened in 1924, the police department consisted of the chief, three desk sergeants, a round sergeant, a detective sergeant, thirteen patrolmen, two traffic officers, a combination patrol car and ambulance, a coupé, and three bicycles, as well as the motorcycle squad. Police telephone numbers were 542 and 438. (Bernie Anderson Sr.)

POLICE CHIEF KEATING, *c.* 1925. Detective Captain George E. Keating (seated here on a Harley-Davidson in front of the Knights of Columbus clubhouse on Main Street) became chief of the Township police on April 5, 1937. He succeeded James A. Walsh who had died suddenly at his home. Chief Keating took an active part in organizing the Woodbridge Defense Council at the start of World War II. He was in charge of the Auxiliary Police and Communications. The Council was formed to consolidate all Township defense efforts at a time when there was great fear in the United States that the war might spread to this country. (Kathy Jost Keating)

AT THE CRACK OF THE BAT, *c.* 1925. The Woodbridge Police Department baseball team looks ready to play ball at the Presbyterian Parish House field on Rahway Avenue. Players are from left to right: (kneeling) Benny Gloff, Rudy Simonsen, George Balint, and Ben Parsons; (standing) Andy Simonsen, Meyer Larsen, Ben Jensen, Leon McElroy, Dan Gibson, and Jack Egan. It is recorded that Township constables were notified on May 4, 1887, to uphold "Blue Laws" which prevented any recreation, including baseball, on Sundays. (Bernie Anderson Sr.)

TALK OF THE TOWN. Shortly after the Woodbridge Fire Company was organized in 1897, the Township raised money to purchase this four-wheel hook and ladder cart. This hose cart could be drawn by either a horse team or by two lines of men pulling on ropes. A hand-drawn fire cart with 400 feet of hose and a dozen fire buckets was an even earlier purchase but was used for only a year.

LA FRANCE COMES TO TOWN, *c.* 1915. Harry Mawbey, one of the first paid firemen, and mascot Nibsy show off the first 750-gallon-per-minute American LaFrance pumper truck. Under that long hood was a big, inline, six-cylinder gasoline engine, with two spark plugs per cylinder for added reliability in moving the vehicle and pumping the water. Each wheel had a solid rubber tire which prevented flats. An American La France booster pumper engine joined the fleet in 1925, and in 1941 the company delivered another pumper truck and a 75-foot aerial ladder truck. (Helen and Janet Mawbey)

ORIGINAL WOODBRIDGE FIREHOUSE, *c.* 1915. The first firehouse constructed entirely of brick, most likely made locally, was built on land purchased for $350 from E.W. Valentine in 1899. The first alarm bell was a steel locomotive wheel tire. The fire hose drying tower at the rear of the building was necessary because hoses were made of a tightly woven canvas cloth and had to be hung to be thoroughly dry. In 1937 the firehouse was remodeled, and in 1967 the building was razed and a new firehouse was built on the site.

ON PARADE, *c.* 1920. Woodbridge Fire Commissioner Frederick H. (Harry) Turner of Sewaren reins in his flag-bedecked horse and carriage during a Memorial Day parade on Green Street, while his grandson Harry R. Howell sits wide-eyed with him in the driver's seat. Unidentified passengers ride in the rear. Mr. Turner owned a paper and twine company in Sewaren. (Todd Howell)

WHITE FIRE TRUCK, *c.* 1924. Every child knows that fire trucks are red, but true to its name, the White Company broke with tradition and painted its fire trucks white! This truck carried men, equipment, and hose to a fire scene provided one of those new-fangled balloon tires didn't have a flat, of course!

FIRELADY, *c.* 1915. Woodbridge resident Stella Kelly strikes a happy pose while trying on a firefighter's hat and raincoat. And with that ax in hand, Miss Kelly appears ready for any emergency! (Helen and Janet Mawbey)

FIREFIGHTERS FOR A DAY, *c.* 1916. The couples on the left are probably sojourning in town—and what better place to visit than the local firehouse with its shiny, spotless equipment, and irresistible gear to try on for a perfect photo opportunity.

AN AMERICAN INSTITUTION, *c.* 1920. With the Stars and Stripes and red, white, and blue bunting flying from every perch, Woodbridge Fire Company No. 1 stands ready for another festive Memorial Day. But there's really no day off for the dedicated firefighters who must always stand ready to answer an emergency alarm.

BOARD OF FIRE COMMISSIONERS, 1924. The gentlemen who served as the civilian governing body of the professional firefighters of Woodbridge Fire District No. 1 are, from left to right, Vice President John Bergen, E.W. Melick, Secretary-Treasurer Peter A. Greiner, President Edward W. Peterson, and Frederick H. Turner. Charles R. Brown, a prominent Township figure, served as fire company president from 1897 until his death in 1939. Another well-known community leader, attorney Leon E. McElroy, succeeded Mr. Brown.

THIRTY GOOD MEN, *c.* 1920. Paid and volunteer firemen line up in front of the Woodbridge Fire House. Behind them stands their Willys-Overland hook and ladder fire truck custom-made by the Perth Amboy Garage in 1915. In service until 1920, the truck had a rear wheel chain-drive, hard rubber tires, and carbide head lamps. And what an adventure to drive! If more than four men stood on the rear platform, the front wheels lifted off the road. Augie Greiner, later Woodbridge mayor, is the second man from the right.

TRAGEDY STRIKES, NOVEMBER 12, 1940. An 8:30 am explosion of unknown origin at the United Railroad Signal Corporation shook the Port Reading section of the Township. The blast injured twenty-five and killed eight people, including Woodbridge resident Dominick LaPenta who worked for the nearby Middlesex Water Company and was in one of its shops when the roof caved in. Since he had been killed one hour after starting work that day, he was paid for that hour only. Mr. LaPenta left his wife, eight young children at home, and several grown sons and daughters. (Frank LaPenta)

Six

Faces and Places

A VICTORIAN PORTRAIT, *c.* 1879. Sarah Anna (seated) and Emily, daughters of Hampton Cutter, the clay mining entrepreneur of Woodbridge, and their gentlemen callers, Freeman Rowland (standing) and James Palmer Prall present a tableau of old-fashioned respectability. Photography at this time required that those having their pictures taken remain still and hold their breath while waiting for the camera to gather enough light to produce an image. (Emily and Margaret Lee)

HIGH ON STRAWBERRY HILL, *c.* 1900. This soaring Township landmark was the residence of the first Hampton Cutter. When his daughter Emily married James Palmer Prall, the couple made their home here. Later the Prall house, as it became known, contained St. Joseph's Orphanage. Today it serves as the headquarters for a nursing service directed by the Little Servant Sisters of the Immaculate Conception. Descendants of the Pralls still live in town.

NELSON FAMILY, *c.* 1893. Four generations of the Nelson family are seated outside their home, one of several houses provided by the W.H. Cutter Clay Mining Co. for its employees. Seated from left to right are great great grandmother Brita Naja Persdotter, Charles Nelson, mother Hannah Larsen Nelson with Oscar Nelson, Frederick Axel Nelson, and great grandmother Anna Louisa Lindquist. Hannah Nelson worked as a maid at the Prall house. Philip Nelson, former Woodbridge resident, descended from this family group. (Rev. Philip Noe Nelson)

CUTTER FAMILY, *c.* 1890. The horses wait patiently for their command to "giddyap" from clay merchant William H. Cutter before trotting off for what was probably a Sunday ride in the family's elegant carriage. Mr. Cutter's wife, the former Sarah R. Barron of town, is seated next to him with daughter Laura in back. Son Hampton looks ready to pedal off to a friend's house. (Emily and Margaret Lee)

CUTTER HOMESTEAD, *c.* 1900. William H. Cutter had this stately home at 123 Green Street built in 1870. His daughter Laura, who died in 1956, lived here all her life. Central Jersey Federal Credit Union now owns the property, and company officials have had the house restored to its original grandeur. For years W.H. Cutter's son Hampton and his wife Edith lived next door at 125 Green Street, still a beautiful residence. (Emily and Margaret Lee)

EDITH A. CUTTER, *c.* 1935. Mrs. Hampton Cutter plays with one of her Persian cats, Blue Boy, in her garden at 125 Green Street. Her husband continued his family's clay mining business and was active in community affairs. Mrs. Cutter was a member of the Tuesday Afternoon Study Club, and the couple both belonged to the Salmagundi Literary and Musical Society of Woodbridge. (Virginia B. Troeger)

JENSEN HOME, *c.* 1910. J.K. Jensen, architect of the original Memorial Municipal Building on Main Street, lived in this 1867 mansion on Green Street at the place where Tisdale Place now intersects. The porte cochere on the right is an attractive example of the covered entrance designed to protect residents and guests from the elements when alighting from their horse-drawn carriages. Mr. Jensen maintained offices at 179 Main and on Smith Street in Perth Amboy.

STREET OF HANDSOME HOUSES, *c.* 1871. Townspeople thought of Green Street as the "residential street of choice" since expansive and expensive Victorian homes lined both sides. The two Greiner homes with their distinctive mansard roofs stand at left and the Dunne house on the right. Township Mayor August F. Greiner maintained his funeral home in the far left Greiner house, a business which continues today as the Greiner-Costello Funeral Home.

M.D. VALENTINE HOME, *c.* 1900. This elegant mansion was one of seven homes on Green Street owned by members of the Valentine family, prompting townsfolk to call them the "Valentine Houses." With its striped awnings and wrap-around veranda, M.D. Valentine's house was obviously built with humid New Jersey summers in mind. Mr. Valentine and his brother James founded the well-known firebrick company which bears their names.

PETER A. GREINER'S BARBER SHOP AND STORE, *c.* 1895. From left to right, an unidentified man, Peter A. Greiner Sr., George Gerdes, and Matthew Stricker pause for a photo outside Greiner's store on Green Street. Located between the railroad and Rahway Avenue, the shop sold a variety of sundries such as shoelaces and buttons, as well as Crescent bicycles, cigars, tobacco, Eastman Kodak cameras, and Edison phonographs and records. Pete was also a barber, shaving and cutting men's hair in his shop and shampooing and trimming ladies' and children's hair in their homes. A story is told that in his old age Pete continued to cut his customers' hair until his death using a magnifying glass. In the mid-1920s a local chapter of the Order of the Eastern Star, a Masonic organization for women, was organized in a rear room of Greiner's shop. Pete Greiner's older son, Peter A. Jr., served as Woodbridge postmaster. His son August, known as Augie, became mayor of Woodbridge in 1933. Mr. Stricker owner of the horse and wagon founded the Gold Medal Coffee and Tea Company on New Street in 1895. He later moved the business to his newly constructed building at 98 Main Street. (Raymond Stricker)

MIDDLESEX COUNTY MOVERS AND SHAKERS, 1951. From left to right, (front) Superior Court Judge and State Senator Bernard W. Vogel, retiring Woodbridge Mayor August Furman Greiner, and former New Jersey Attorney General David T. Wilentz, (back) Township Tax Collector Michael J. Trainer, and Woodbridge Mayor-elect Hugh B. Quigley pause for a photo at Mayor Greiner's retirement celebration after eighteen years in office. Township Historian Ruth Wolk described this event in her *History of Woodbridge, New Jersey*: "In December the Woodbridge Jewish Center was packed to its capacity for a banquet given to pay homage to Mayor Greiner. Republicans and Democrats alike joined in the tribute. Charles E. Gregory served as toastmaster and David T. Wilentz was principal speaker. The guest of honor was the recipient of many gifts." Mr. Vogel, a respected public figure, was affectionately known as "the judge." Mr. Wilentz built a large law firm in Perth Amboy and is remembered as the prosecuting attorney at the world-famous Lindbergh kidnapping trial in 1935. Mr. Greiner, a 32nd Degree Mason and owner and director of Greiner's Funeral Home, provided stability and hope to his people during the Great Depression and World War II. A Shell Oil plant manager for forty years, Mr. Quigley was mayor from 1952 to 1959 and guided Woodbridge at a time of postwar growth, while Mr. Trainer garnered the faith of the voters who gave him tenure of office as tax collector.

MASONIC HALL, *c.* 1900. Americus Lodge No. 83 of the Free and Accepted Masons was incorporated here on the third floor of this large Green Street building around February 1870 with William T. Ames, Isaac Inslee, William B. Reed, Charles C. Dalley, Robert J. Wylie, Charles M. Dally, and Daniel W. Brown as charter members. Township Attorney Ephraim Cutter maintained his law office on the second floor.

OLD TIME EMPORIUM. E. Peterson's shop opened about 1900 on the street level of the Masonic Hall. The store sold jewelry, sundry items, and bicycles and also repaired watches. The wooden figure of a Native American on the right would be a prized antique store item today. Years later when the Masons moved to the Craftsmen's Club, the Township newspaper, *The Independent-Leader*, moved into this building. (Madeline LaPenta Peterson)

RAINBOW GIRLS, SEPTEMBER 1946. The charter members of the Americus Chapter, Order of the Rainbow for Girls, were initiated into the organization at the Craftsmen's Club on Green Street which continued as their meeting place. Mrs. Robert J. Graham (seated center) served as Mother Advisor. The Rainbow Girls is an international organization affiliated with the Masons and the Order of the Eastern Star. The Woodbridge chapter continued for many years but finally disbanded. (Virginia B. Troeger)

A CONTINUING BUSINESS, *c.* 1906. From left to right, Barney Dunigan, Owen S. Dunigan, John Brown, and Harry Mawbey pause outside Edgar and Dunigan's plumbing and heating business on Rahway Avenue. (The man on right is unidentified.) In 1887 Owen Dunigan, at age 15, apprenticed with Edwin Zimmerman, who founded the company. Businessmen Frank Edgar Sr. and Jr. invested in the shop, but eventually Owen Dunigan became sole owner. When he died in 1957, his son, Richard, ran the business until he retired in 1992 and sold it to James Juarez. (Dick Dunigan)

PIKE HOUSE, *c.* 1900. Myth surrounds this early landmark on the corner of Green Street and Rahway Avenue. Some say it was called the Pike House because the turnpike to Rahway and Carteret passed by its door. Others think it was named in honor of Zebulon Pike, the discoverer of Pike's Peak whose grandfather was a noted local resident. Town meetings were held here from 1849 to 1874. Later known as the Woodbridge Hotel or the King Hotel, the old Pike House was demolished in the 1930s.

RIDING THE RAILS, *c.* 1900. The Pennsylvania Railroad carried passengers from the Woodbridge station at Pearl Street northbound to Newark and New York City and southbound to Perth and South Amboy and the Jersey shore. Through the years steam engines have yielded to electric locomotives, and the old Pennsylvania has changed names several times (it is now New Jersey Transit). Built in 1885, this station was demolished in 1939.

GREEN STREET GRADE CROSSING, *c.* 1930. After many decades Woodbridge residents fought long and hard for elevated railroad tracks. In 1935 gatekeeper John Shannon died and engineer Albert Terhune was also killed when his train hit a Shell Oil gasoline truck here. Township officials joined New Jersey Public Utility Commissioner Harry Bachrach to obtain funds from Washington. Finally in 1938 Assistant Secretary of the Navy Charles Edison obtained financial backing for the job.

CELEBRATING SAFETY, MAY 20, 1940. Crowds gather on Pearl Street for a momentous day in Woodbridge—the celebration of the new elevated railroad station built at the exact location of the old one and the new elevated railroad tracks. The Pennsylvania Railroad tracks were elevated at five Woodbridge intersections: Main, Green, and Freeman Streets, Valentine's Fire Brick Company, and Factory Lane. However, in Avenel where Avenel Street crosses the tracks at street level, the roadway was redesigned to pass underneath the railroad.

FLORISTS, *c.* 1925. Anna Rohde Baldwin and her husband Fred owned the Woodbridge Florist Shoppe on Rahway Avenue for many years. The couple sold their store in 1945 to John C. Schwarz who operated it until his death in 1963. The business continues under the same name at the same place with John's son, Richard C. Schwarz, now the owner. (Richard C. Schwarz)

DR. FREEMAN'S HOMESTEAD, *c.* 1880. This is an artist's drawing of a grand Italianate structure owned by Woodbridge physician Ellis B. Freeman. Dr. Freeman served as one of the original trustees of the Barron Free Public Library and a trustee of the First Presbyterian Church. Later J.H. Thayer Martin, the Township attorney, and his wife inherited the house, which was torn down about 1950 to make room for the Woodbridge Apartments.

THE BARRON FREE PUBLIC LIBRARY, *c.* 1900. An architectural treasure built in the Romanesque Revival style, the Barron Library, now the Barron Arts Center, appears today almost exactly as in this photograph. The library was built with funds bequeathed by Woodbridge native Thomas Barron, who was born in 1790. Mr. Barron and a partner formed a trading company in New Orleans to deal in the West Indies. Later Mr. Barron bought out his partner and amassed a fortune from his trading house. Mr. Barron never married and retired to New York City in 1827 to devote his time to study, philanthropy, and fishing. He never forgot Woodbridge, however, and stipulated in his will that $50,000 be used to build a free public library and reading room in the town of his birth. Dr. John C. Barron of New York, who was Thomas Barron's nephew and executor of his will, donated property from the Barron estate for the library, which opened on September 11, 1877. Many architectural details are visible on the facade and inside this exquisitely designed structure. Important interior features include a rose window and a fireplace embellished with blue and white Delft tiles from Holland which portray Biblical motifs. A century after it was built, the library was placed on the State and National Registers of Historical Places.

JOHN C. BARRON, M.D., *c.* 1880. Nephew of the Barron Library benefactor, Thomas Barron, and executor of his will, Dr. John Barron was born in Woodbridge in 1837. A graduate of the College of Physicians and Surgeons in New York City, he served as a surgeon with the United States Army during the Civil War and later as surgeon-general of the New York National Guard, holding the rank of colonel. His extensive travels in later life included a 700-mile adventure up the Nile River.

JANNI'S SWEET SHOP, *c.* 1940. Richard Janni smiles for his customers behind the counter of his confectionery store on the corner of Rahway Avenue and Green Street. Opened by Richard's father about 1930, Janni's was an institution in this part of town, patronized by young and old. From 1948 until 1987 Mr. Janni owned and operated the Village Inn on the site of his former sweet shop.

TRINITY CHURCH, *c.* 1900. The Episcopalians of Woodbridge can trace their history to around 1698. Trinity cemetery dates back to 1714, with the earliest remaining headstone marked 1750. The present Trinity Church completed in 1860 stands on the foundations of two earlier churches. During the 1750s James Parker, who printed the first newspaper in New Jersey, served as lay reader for the congregation. In 1777 British and Hessian troops based in Woodbridge commandeered the second Trinity Church to use as their barracks. After an earlier minister's house was sold in 1872, the Jonathan Dunham homestead (1670) which adjoins the church was purchased and restored for use as the minister's house. The historic Dunham dwelling continues to serve as the rectory for Trinity Church.

THE OLD WHITE CHURCH (DATE UNKNOWN). This widely recognized Woodbridge landmark, the First Presbyterian Church, is pictured here as it looked in 1804. This building was erected on the site of an earlier church and meetinghouse, built in 1675. To date there has been a church on this site for more than 320 years. During the Revolutionary War (1775–1783), the Reverend Azel Roe was captured by the British for preaching the cause of liberty and imprisoned for a time at the Old Sugar House in New York City.

PRESBYTERIAN CEMETERY, *c.* 1900. This historic graveyard adjoining the First Presbyterian Church encompasses a veritable "Who's Who" of early Woodbridge settlers. Weathered gravestones mark the final resting places of members of the Freeman, Barron, Edgar, Prall, Harned, Bloomfield, and Fitz Randolph families, Revolutionary soldiers, five ministers of the church, and the first child born in Woodbridge, Mary Compton Campbell(1667–1734). (Don Aaroe)

REVOLUTIONARY WAR MEMORIAL, 1927. Members of the Daughters of the American Revolution or D. A. R., (from left) Mrs. Frank Valentine, regent of the Janet Gage Chapter in Woodbridge; Mrs. Banks, National Vice President General; and Mrs. Becker, State Regent; dedicate a monument "In memory of the Revolutionary Soldiers and Patriots of Woodbridge, New Jersey" near the Presbyterian Church. After the Janet Gage Chapter closed because of declining membership, the monument was removed, but the plaque has been saved for future display.

CHILDREN OF THE AMERICAN REVOLUTION, 1927. Wearing dainty white dresses and corsages, these local young ladies must have enjoyed an eventful day as participants in the D.A.R. monument dedication. (See photo above) They are, from left to right: Evelyn Kreger, Olive Spencer, Elizabeth Baker, Jane Warr, Barbara Stern, Eleanor Harned, Adelaide Harned, Jean Kreger, Betty Copeland, Grace Moffett, Norma Chase, Jane Copeland, and an unidentified child at far right. (Jean Bowers Jost)

"MCEWEN'S CORNER," *c.* 1898. Until St. George Avenue was realigned at a later time, all traffic from Rahway passed the Joseph McEwen home, aptly called "McEwen's Corner." Grouped on the decorative porch of the house which still stands are, from left to right: local mason and contractor Joseph McEwen Sr., daughter Marion, his wife Mary Treen McEwen, his father-in-law John Treen Sr., and daughters Agnes and Amy. Joseph McEwen Jr. and dog Bruno stand in the foreground.

JOST-KEATING HOUSE, *c.* 1950. This red Colonial home on Freeman Street, earlier known as the Aaron Dunn homestead, is one of Woodbridge's oldest existing houses. Lovingly restored by Norbert Jost and his late wife, Edna Oberlies Jost, the house is now the residence of their daughter and son-in-law, Kathy and Ned Keating. It may have served as the home of an early minister of the Presbyterian church. (Kathy Jost Keating)

RIDGEDALE AVENUE HOME, *c.* 1840. This small gem of a house captures elements of the Gothic Revival style. The residence, which is still occupied, was built for a Mr. Woodward seated here in his buggy. At the time of Mr. Woodward's death in 1897, his sister, a Mrs. Lamb (at right), moved into the house. Other owners included Nicholas and Marie Younger, who sold the house in 1968. (Nancy Younger Dunham)

EDGAR R.R. STATION, *c.* 1920. A local station between Woodbridge and Avenel, Edgar was a popular stop for racing fans during the years of the Woodbridge Speedway. When the Pennsylvania Railroad wanted to purchase land from Frank Edgar of Edgar's Hill around 1867, Mr. Edgar agreed to sell only if the railroad would build a station on the property. Mr. Edgar presumably wanted his son to ride the train to Stevens Institute of Technology in Hoboken. The station later burned down, and trains no longer stop at Edgar.

CHRISTENSEN BROTHERS. Chris Christensen (left), *c.* 1925, and his brother, John Peter, shown with his bride, Bertha Anderson, *c.* 1905, came to Woodbridge from Denmark. Both tailors, the brothers opened their first department store on Main Street in 1895, which is probably the oldest family retail business in the Township. Later Chris's sons Gilford and Herbert and his son-in-law Howard Macnab managed the store. Herbert and his family are still affiliated with the business.

WATER METER READER, *c.* 1910. Not everyone had water supplied by the Middlesex Water Company at this time, so it's a good bet this horse knew which buildings to pass as he pulled William Nixon Eborn in his buckboard on meter reading rounds. And chances are William rarely had to remove the whip from its holder, especially on the homestretch. An ideal summer position, but in the chill of winter Bill Eborn must have had thoughts of getting an inside job! (Middlesex Water Company)

SMALL FRY WEDDING, 1932. Mock weddings for youngsters, also called Tom Thumb weddings, were a popular event in past years and were often sponsored by churches and schools as a means of raising money. With such a large "wedding party," this gala affair held at the First Congregational Church on Barron Avenue must have required countless rehearsals. From left to right, the cast members are: (front row) Elizabeth Ostrom, Hugh Burgess, Margaret Hramotnik, Lela Copeland, Virginia Wight, Jerry Jardot, Robert Hooban, Geraldine Hooban, Alex Baka, Nancy Lou Jernee, Arthur Kovach, and John Raison, who is seated in front; (second row) Robert Osterland, Elizabeth Hramotnik, Malcolm Mosher, Emily Lou Holland, Joyce Morgenson, Gorham Boynton, Barbara Burgess, Robert Keating, Ruth Trautwein, George Rothweiler, Betty Jane Killenberger, Carolyn Hall, William Lauritsen, and Shermer Bussinger; (third row) Charlotte Webb, Beverly Raison, John Mesar, Michael Serak, Barbara Serak, Charles Kurta, Helen Seyglinski, Joseph Seyglinski, Patricia Anderson, Melvin Raison, Marguery Johnson, John Hramotnik, director Miss Grace Switzer, Margaret Lauritsen, Esther Baka, and Olga Kovach; (back row) Gloria Hall, Elsie Vargo, Harry Linde, Philip Nelson, Stanley Seyglinski, Vivian Raison, Virginia Ostrom, and Evelyn Simm. (Rev. Philip Noe Nelson)

MOTHER AND CHILD, 1862. Mrs. Jacob C. Ashley holds her daughter Etta in this vintage photograph. Etta would later marry John Treen Jr., uniting two old New Jersey families. This photo may have been a ferrotype or a tintype, a positive photograph made on a sensitized sheet of enameled iron or tin.

"SAY CHEESE," *c*. 1885. John Treen Jr. and Etta Ashley Treen pose for a portrait not long after they were married. A newspaper account reported their November 12, 1884 wedding as follows: "Our friend and townsman, Mr. John Treen, Jr., was married to Miss Etta A., daughter of Mr. Jacob C. Ashley, at the residence of the bride's father, last evening, Rev. J.H. Runyon, officiating. The bride was attended by two little ladies—her sister, Miss Mary Ashley and Miss Elsie Lawson—as bridesmaids. Mr. and Mrs. Treen will please accept our congratulations upon the happy event."

MARTIN G. ASHLEY, 1925. Etta Ashley Treen's brother proudly displays his Model T Ford on Grove Street. In 1911 Mr. Ashley, a real estate agent, was named recorder, or magistrate, of Woodbridge Township. At this time the recorder did not need a law degree, and from all accounts, Mr. Ashley served successfully without one. Not one of his more than 15,000 judicial decisions was overturned by a higher court. In 1927 Bernard W. Vogel succeeded Mr. Ashley.

JOHN TREEN JR., *c.* 1925. John Treen and his wife, Etta, made their home at 169 Grove Street. Their three children, William, Charles, and Mabel, also spent their lives at the family residence. A mason and builder Mr. Treen served as the Township building inspector and as a leader of the local Masonic Order. In her later years Etta Treen's sister, Mary L. Ashley, a dressmaker, lived with the Treens.

MABEL ELIZABETH TREEN, *c.* 1915. Miss Treen was right in fashion with her middy blouse outfit, which derived its name from a shortened form of "midshipman." Miss Treen taught school in Newark and was a beloved member of the community and of the Woodbridge Methodist Church, where she often sang solos in the choir. A garden has been named in her memory on the church property.

LONGTIME CITIZEN, *c.* 1950. Charles H. Kuhlman's life spanned much of the twentieth century. Although born in Brooklyn in 1895, he lived in Woodbridge for most of his life. Mr. Kuhlman, who died in 1992, served with the U.S. Army Lightning Division in France during World War I. He was a charter member of American Legion Post No. 87 and the last surviving member of the Post's Last Man's Club. He and his wife, Marion, raised two children, John and Howard, who still live in the area with their families.

VENERABLE CLERGYMAN, *c.* 1950. The Right Reverend Monsignor Charles G. McCorristin served as pastor of St. James Roman Catholic Church from 1937 until his death in 1966. In 1948 His Holiness, Pope Pius XII, appointed Father McCorristin a domestic prelate, with the title of Right Reverend Monsignor.

ST. JAMES' STAFF, *c.* 1945. Sisters of Mercy (from left to right) Daniel, Florien, Judith, Raphael, Mary Hugh, Begniga, Consuella, Paulette, David, Josephus, and Martinas, Father Maurice P. Griffin, Father Napoleon, and Father Charles G. McCorristin gather for a dinner at St. James School on Amboy Avenue. In 1990 the school celebrated its 100th anniversary, "a century of excellence" in providing a Catholic education to area children.

THE GANG'S ALL HERE, *c.* 1900. Woodbridge gentlemen enjoying the festivities at a local picnic are, from left to right: Pete Jensen (wearing apron), Henry Lew (behind Pete wearing hat), Randy Lee (with bottle on head), John Leisen (wearing straw hat), Arthur Berry (wearing vest), John Brown, Maurice P. Dunigan (holding bottle), Thomas F. Dunigan (seated in white shirt), Owen S. Dunigan, unidentified man behind Owen, Richard Sattler (seated with hat in hand), Edward Cohen (behind Richard), unidentified man (wearing vest and chain), Patrick Murphy, Jack Gerity (on far right), and William Irvine (seated in foreground). (Dick Dunigan)

THE BOYS OF SUMMER, 1900. The highly successful Woodbridge Athletic Association played both amateur and professional baseball teams around the state. The players are, from left to right: (front row) David Brown and Jim Watt; (second row) Frank Cohen, Gus Simmons, Art Brown, and George Stimets; (third row) Will Anness, Fred Brown, and Charles Brown; (back row) manager John Ferris and Bill Brown.

SUMMER OUTING, AUGUST 1927. Woodbridge friends (from left to right) Helen and Gertrude Pfeiffer, Albert Bergen, Mabel Treen, Helen Ensign, and Mr. Bergen's brother- in-law Clayton Duval, together with Miriam Bergen who took this snapshot, enjoy a day at Culver's Lake, New Jersey. The Misses Pfeiffer were daughters of John Pfeiffer, plant superintendent at the Valentine Fire Brick Co. Miss Ensign's father, Everett, was the clerk of the Board of Education for thirty-five years. (Virginia B. Troeger)

"TAKE IT FROM THE TOP!" Robert J. McEwen (right front) and his "Rhythm Kings" make music at Woodbridge High School in 1941. Musicians are, from left to right: Fred Brause, Ed Zullo, George Ryan, George Parsler, Guy Weaver, Henry Larsen, Robert Stephen, McEwen, Dick Murphy, and Dorothy Langan. George Parseler and Guy Weaver were fatalities of World War II. Ed Zullo is a dentist on Main Street. Now known as Dory Previn, Dorothy Langan was the soloist and string bass player with the band. Today she is a well-known lyricist and was formerly married to André Previn, the conductor and composer.

JEAN MERRILL, 1945. Jean, pictured here on her front steps, was the younger daughter of Township Engineer George R. Merrill and his wife Ethel Sims Merrill of Elmwood Avenue. Mr. Merrill later served as the Middlesex County engineer, supervising county road and bridge construction until his death in 1944. Merrill Park in Colonia was named in his memory. Jean Merrill married Bruce Rankin of Sewaren at the First Presbyterian Church in the late 1940s. (Virginia B. Troeger)

BY THE BROOK, *c.* 1925. From left to right, George Lattanzio, Madeline LaPenta Peterson, and her husband Earle pause at Heard's Brook on School Street. Since Woodbridge Park had not been developed at this time, Heard's (also spelled Hurd's) Brook still ran wild and often flooded the area during heavy rains.(Madeline LaPenta Peterson)

Seven

The Speedway

WOODBRIDGE SPEEDWAY, *c.* 1930. Thrill-seeking crowds packed "The World's Fastest Half-Mile Race Track" in Woodbridge every other Sunday, May through September from 1927 to 1938. The track, located on the present site of Woodbridge High School on Kelly Street, was originally made of wooden boards, but through the years they rotted and were replaced in 1933 by a oiled dirt track. The excitement of these races was often intense and the noise ear-splitting. Without mufflers, the engine exhaust could be heard all the way to Main Street.

How To Get To Woodbridge Track By Auto

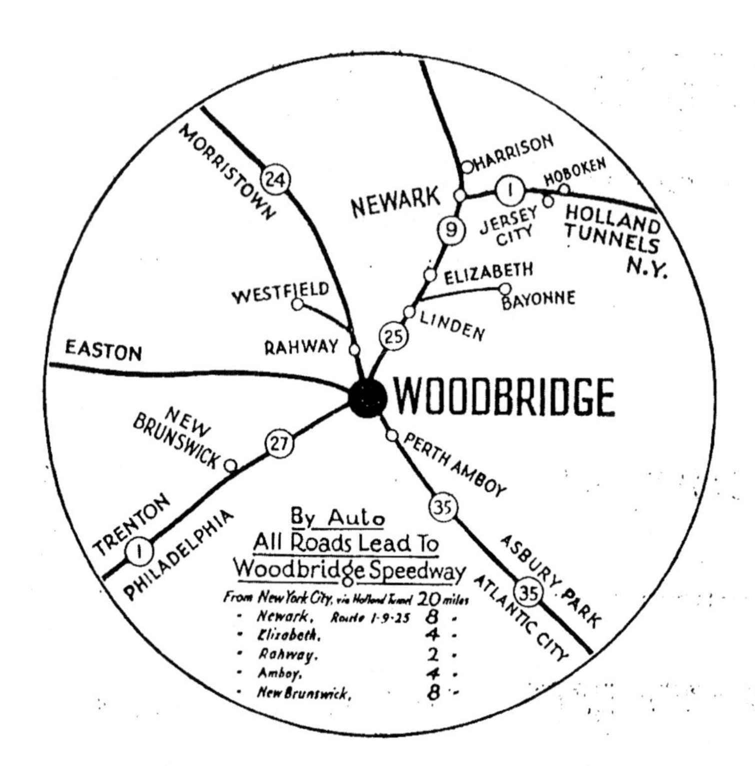

Pennsylvania Railroad Runs Special Trains To Track

Special trains over the Pennsylvania Railroad are run to the Woodbridge automobile races every Sunday. Special round trip fares are charged and the specials will run every Sunday up to and including, Sunday, October 22nd.

The train leaves the Pennsylvania railroad depot and makes stops at Manhattan Transfer to pick up passengers coming through the Hudson Tubes, at Newark and at Elizabeth, stopping at the Edgar Station, which is directly in back of the Grandstand of the track.

From New York, at the Hudson Terminal, the round trip fare is 90 cents and from the Pennsylvania up-town station at 34th Street, $1.05. The round trip fare from Newark is 55 cents and the same from Elizabeth 35 cents.

The tickets are sold for Train No. 787, leaving New York at 1:35 P.M., arriving at Edgar at 2:19 P.M. in time to see some of the time trials, which begin at 1.00 P.M. Returning the tickets are good on Train No. 786, scheduled to leave Edgar at 6:01. The time of the trains from Newark to the track will be 1:52 P.M. and Elizabeth 2:00 P.M.

ALL ROADS LEAD TO . . . , *c.* 1933. Easy access made it possible for thousands of people to attend the auto races at the Woodbridge Speedway, years before the Garden State Parkway and the New Jersey Turnpike converged at Woodbridge.

STARTING POSITIONS, *c.* 1930. Based on a point system involving number of races, position at finish, fastest lap time, and other factors, a car and driver were assigned a starting position. Each crew pushed its car into position and waited, hoping all was in readiness. Then a track official probably announced, "Gentlemen, start your engines," which meant that a mechanic had to spin the hand crank. If all drivers held their positions for a pace lap, they would be off to a flying start when the green flag came down. (John Kozub)

THE TEAM, *c.* 1932. Standing, from left to right, are car owner Lew Krosak, mechanics Harold Deter and Paul Kimball, and driver Bryan Saulspaugh, who was killed a few years later making a time trial at a West Coast track.

CROWD PLEASER, JULY 27, 1930. Popular driver Bob Robinson of Daytona Beach, Florida, views the track with Ralph A. Hankinson of Woodcliffe, New Jersey, the director general of the Speedway.

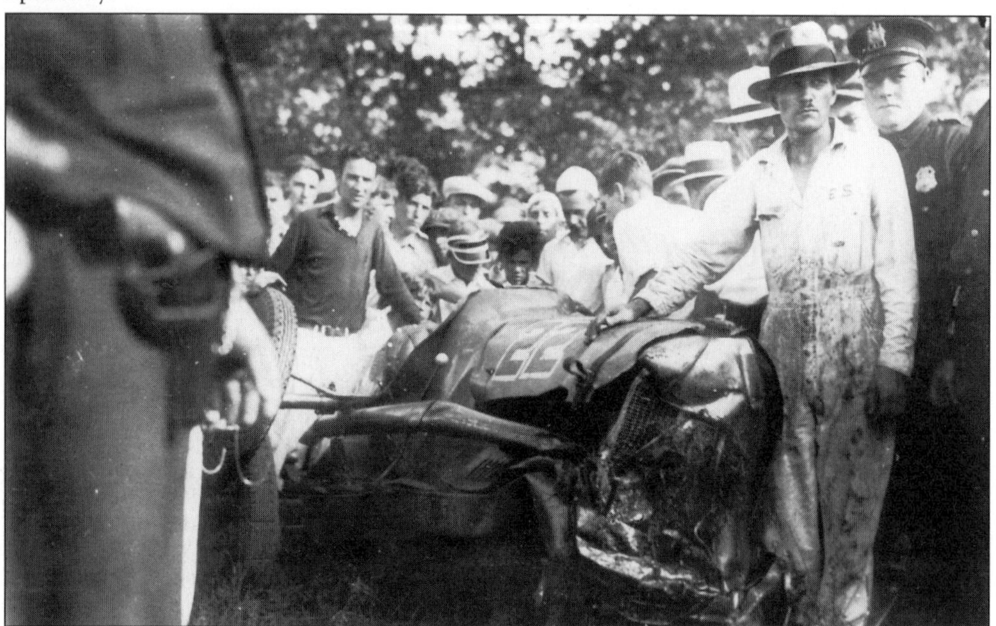

SAD ENDING, JULY 27, 1930. Bob Robinson had just triumphed in two races before his fatal crash. He and another driver Rick Decker of Staten Island, New York, were vying for first place when Decker's car blew a front tire forcing Robinson up against the outer guardrail, which then collapsed. Still in his car, Robinson was thrown over the stands hitting a tree outside the track. Some years later after Decker's death, another account of Robinson's accident was released. It stated that Decker was suddenly stung by a bee or wasp which caused him to swerve into Robinson.

ACCIDENT SPECTATORS, JULY 27, 1930. Bob Robinson's fatal crash caused extensive damage to the old wooden guard railing, viewed here from the outside of the race track. As a result, the management had a strong steel cable installed around the perimeter of the track. (John Kozub)

SPECTATORS' VIEW, *c.* 1930. For the high price of $1.75, a fan could view the races from one of these wooden chairs in the grandstand, and for $1.50, a fan could mingle with the race crews in the center of the oval or sit in the bleachers. (John Kozub)

WOODBRIDGE WINNER, JUNE 1929. Lou Moore, a Los Angeles racer, smiles from his Miller Majestic Special for his many fans after finishing first in a race. (John Kozub)

TROPHY MAN, *c.* 1930. Fred Frame from Los Angeles, a very winning driver, exhibits some of his trophies. The impressive-looking cup on the right presented to him by Esso Oil Company was surely one of his tallest, measuring approximately 3 feet in height. (John Kozub)

PROGRAM COVER, *c*. 1930.

CRASH, *c*. 1933. Two unidentified drivers collide on the track. No information is available on the outcome.

MASCOT, AUGUST 1933. Mechanic and test driver Harold Deter clowns around with the Speedway's mascot, a spotted pig. Driver Johnny Gerber gives the pig a friendly tweak while a bemused Maynard Clark, dubbed "the Adonis of the Speedway" in a program commentary, watches. (John Kozub)

SPECTACULAR FINISH, *c.* 1933. Notice the empty space under the hood where the engine was completely blown out of this Tee Lynn Ambler. Lucky, lucky day! No injuries reported here.

UP, UP, AND AWAY, 1934. Jack Erickson of Roselle, New Jersey, won't be going far in his Hal Special. The right front wheel has just broken off and can be seen in the air behind his car. No report on the outcome.

THE DIRT TRACK, MAY 28, 1933. The boards are gone. The track is dirt. The car is a Fronty Special. The driver is Joe Miller. And a tow truck stands ready at track side. Spectators at dirt track races left for home covered with a fine brown dust which most of them proudly wore as the badge of a true fan.

HEADQUARTERS FOR RACINIG DRIVERS
AFTER EACH RACE

RESERVATIONS
PHONE: WOODBRIDGE 8-2391

WANA'S

LOCATED AT WOODBRIDGE

ON SHORE HIGHWAY AT THE SPEEDWAY

The Same As Last Year

SANDWICHES, SODA
AND REFRESHMENTS

$1.50 CHICKEN, STEAK
OR CHOP DINNERS

DINE and DANCE

MAMMOTH GIRLIE REVUE

NO COVER CHARGE AT ANY TIME

WANA'S, *c.* 1935. Wana's was a great place to relax after the stress of the races, and the "Mammoth Girlie Revue" surely cheered winners and losers alike. Robin's Inn was another popular restaurant near the track. By the mid-1930s, the Great Depression had caused massive unemployment and falling prices, and Speedway attendance waned. Ticket prices were dropped; floodlights were installed for night racing, but the crowds just weren't there anymore. Woodbridge Speedway closed forever after the 1938 season.

Eight

Touring the Township

HOP ON THE BUS, 1927. Owner Joseph Horvath of Perth Amboy stands in the doorway of his "City Bus Line" bus with driver William Vereb. The line operated between Perth Amboy and Carteret with stops in Woodbridge and Chrome, a section of Carteret. Family-owned jitneys, as these small vehicles were often called, were forced out of business as Public Service and later New Jersey Transit consolidated the independent routes.

MEN OF READING COAL, SUMMER 1893. Employees of the Reading Coal Company are assembled at the Pier No. One coal dock in Port Reading in front of the yard office building. They are, from left to right: (front row) unidentified man; Captain Shoe, shore captain in charge of tugs and barges; John Goff, stenographer; Larry Barrett, first superintendent of Port Reading Yard; Charles Farrell, assistant superintendent; and unidentified; (second row) Al Bitting; unidentified; Walter Blair; Charles Penrose; Joseph R. Neveil Jr.; Walter Douglas; William Johnson; James Garrity; Jess Wilson; James Duffy at rear; Tom Mulvilhill in front; unidentified; Captain Conley; and unidentified. Tom Mulvihill was later elected mayor of Carteret, serving for sixteen years. Joseph Neveil Jr. held the job of engineer on the first coal train to enter Port Reading Terminal. At right is a Philadelphia and Reading Railway Co. (later renamed Reading Railway Co.) coal car awaiting its turn to be moved.

COMPANY HEADQUARTERS, 1950. The public image of a company is often formed from a look at the building in which it functions. A tall, solid, imposing structure built of brick and stone and completed in the early 1900s, the Port Reading terminal of the Reading Company projected strength and stability. Buying and selling coal was the business of the Reading Company, a leader in its field.

COAL DUMPER, 1950. As the name implies, the Port Reading Terminal was the end of the line for railroad coal cars headed for the Reading Company, who bought coal out of state and had it shipped here. Visible between the tracks is a four-wheeled device called a "pig," which was connected to a loaded coal car to move it to the top of a ramp. Next a special machine turned the car over and in less than a minute dumped the entire load into a waiting barge. Ultimately tugs hauled the barges to electrical generating plants where the coal fueled the steam boilers.

THE CLOVERLEAF, *c.* 1925. The four-leaf clover configuration of this sprawling intersection of Route 25 and Route Four (now Routes One and 35/St. George Avenue) is clearly visible in this aerial view. One of the first such traffic circles in the country, the Woodbridge Cloverleaf has remained virtually unchanged, but plans are in progress to rebuild it in the late 1990s.

FORMER FORDS LIBRARY. Originally the Redeemer Lutheran Chapel, this building, shown in a recent photo, was donated by the Lutheran Church to the Woman's Club of Fords in 1940 to house the Fords Public Library. From 1924 to 1940, the club maintained a library for the townspeople in various rented quarters and were delighted to have a permanent library at last. In the 1960s the Fords Library became a branch of the Woodbridge Township Library and was later moved to a new site. This building continues as the headquarters of the Woman's Club of Fords. (Mary Molnar)

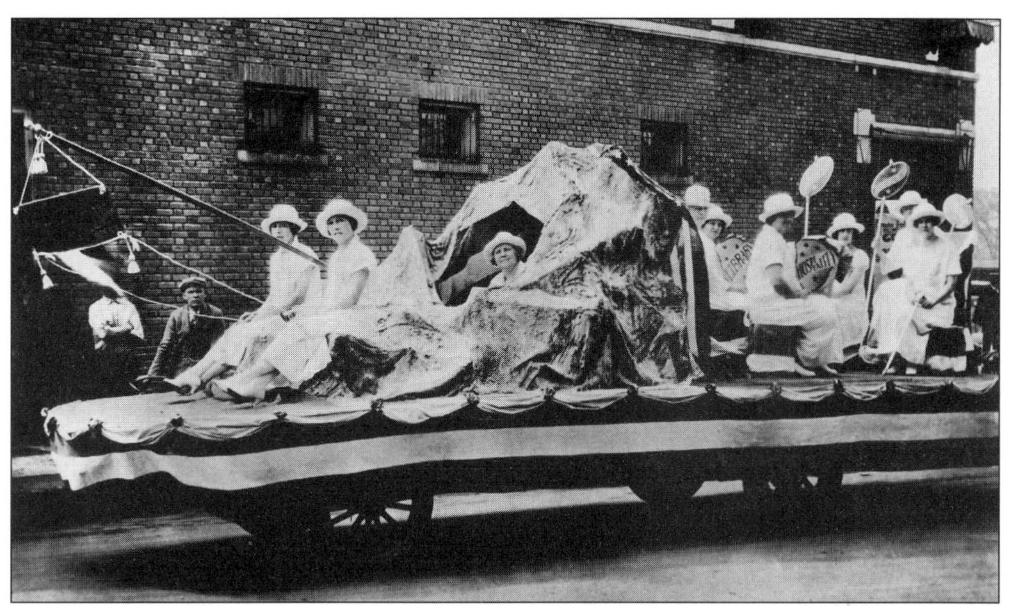

WINNING FLOAT, JUNE 14, 1924. The Women's Club of Fords was awarded a cup for their gala parade float at the Woodbridge Memorial Municipal Building dedication and 255th Township anniversary celebration. The ladies are, from left to right: Mrs. William Lybeck, Mrs. Liddle Esche, Mrs. Albert Weismann, Mrs. Hiram Ward, Mrs. Mulford Mills, Mrs. Viggo Ferdinandsen, Ms. Howard Madison, Mrs. George Liddle, and Mrs. Willard Dunham. (Mary Molnar)

"FILL 'ER UP," *c.* 1930. Chances are though that in these early Depression years motorists couldn't afford a full tank of gas. They probably pulled up to the curb at Lund's Service Station for a dollar's worth. Located on New Brunswick Avenue in Fords, Lund's carried Lee tires and tubes, Tydol gasoline, and Fada radios—and, road maps were free, of course!

AN ISELIN CHURCH, *c.* 1925. Back in 1850 the First Presbyterian Church started as the Union Chapel in Uniontown, which was Iselin's earlier name. The chapel was located on the present site of the Iselin Fire Company. When the original chapel burned about 1920, the members built a new church at the corner of Oak Tree Road and Route 27. It was known as the Union Non-denominational Chapel of Iselin until 1933 when it became the First Presbyterian Church of Iselin. (Betty Stauffer)

ENTERTAINMENT, *c.* 1963. A double feature is posted at the Iselin Theatre: *The Condemned of Altona*, starring Sophia Loren, Maximillian Schell, Frederic March, and Robert Wagner and *Take Her, She's Mine* with James Stewart and Sandra Dee. However, for those who'd rather stay home, they could rent a TV next door according to a small sign in the side window. (Betty Stauffer)

AVENEL LIBRARY, *c.* 1930. In 1926 Avenel residents Mr. and Mrs. John B. La Bat donated land at 236–238 Avenel Street for the Free Public Library of Avenel. The following year this quaint wooden building, 14 feet wide and 20 feet long, opened to the public with Mr. La Bat serving as president of the Board of Trustees. This tiny library, which may have been the smallest in the state, no longer exists since a larger library was built in 1958 at the same location.

ALONG ROUTE 25, AVENEL, *c.* 1930. Small roadside stands, such as Hiram's (right), sold fresh vegetables and fruits along the Avenel stretch of Route 25, now Route One. Much of the produce was grown elsewhere and trucked to Avenel. One owner made regular trips to Florida to supply his stand with fresh oranges, grapefruits, and lemons. (Bernie Anderson Sr.)

WORLD WAR I HOSPITAL, 1918. When Colonia resident and orthopedic surgeon, Dr. Fred H. Albee, was named director of a proposed hospital for veterans requiring orthopedic treatment, he began a search for a suitable location. Enter another Colonia resident Charles D. Freeman, who was a member of the New York Cotton Exchange. Mr. Freeman offered to lease 200 acres of his estate for the hospital, and Dr. Albee promptly persuaded the U.S. Army to build USA General Hospital No. 3 in Colonia. (Robert Rippen)

HOSPITAL FIRE DEPARTMENT, 1918. With an American LaFrance fire engine in the firehouse on the grounds of USA General Hospital No. 3 in Colonia, the tone was set that no expense would be spared to establish this complex, which took only a few months to build. (Robert Rippen)

THE WOUNDED, *c.* 1918. Returning veterans from "the war to end all wars" who required orthopedic treatment for their injuries were hospitalized here at the USA General Hospital in Colonia. Dr. Fred H. Albee, Colonia resident and hospital director, performed many of the bone graft operations. Out of six thousand servicemen treated, only seventeen died at the hospital.

PHYSICAL THERAPY BUILDING, COLONIA, *c.* 1918. USA General Hospital No. 3 included 110 barracks-type buildings with eighteen single-story wards, five mess halls and kitchens, a central heating plant, telephone exchange, swimming pool, libraries, and a newspaper named *Over Here*. The hospital existed for only fifteen months. On October 15, 1919, the Army closed General Hospital No. 3 and later razed most of the buildings. (Robert Rippen)

"BLYTHMOOR," COLONIA, *c.* 1915. Dr. Fred Houdlett Albee, chief surgeon at USA General Hospital No. 3 in Colonia, maintained this imposing mansion, another home in Venice, Florida, and his medical office at 57 West 57th Street, New York City. "Blythmoor's" many amenities included a built-in pipe organ, the largest dining room in Colonia, a swimming pool, and in true Victorian style, a conservatory. After receiving his medical degree in 1903 from Harvard, Dr. Albee specialized in orthopedics and in 1906 performed the first bone graft operation. Through the years his reputation grew as a result of his teaching, lectures, writing, and, of course, his pioneering bone graft procedures. In 1943 Dr. Albee wrote his autobiography *A Surgeon's Fight to Rebuild Men*, which included an introduction by Lowell Thomas, the famous radio commentator. Dr. Albee received many honors throughout his life. He was named Chevalier of the Legion of Honor in France, Cavaliere of the Order of the Crown in Italy, and Grand Officer of the Southern Cross in Brazil, among others. He was a member of the Sons of the American Revolution, the Barnegat Hunting and Fishing Club, and the Colonia Country Club where he served as president in 1914–1915. Born in 1876, Dr. Albee died at the age of 69 after a short illness. The home was razed in the 1980s and a number of homes have been built on the property.

COLONIA COUNTRY CLUB, *c.* 1899. In 1890 New York businessman Edward K. Cone and family moved to a colonial house called "The Trees" on 60 acres in Houghtonville, now Colonia. Mr. Cone developed several homes on his land and named them "The Colony." To enhance the elegance of the community, Mr. Cone and others purchased an additional 50 acres to build a nine-hole golf course, which opened in 1899. The Adams homestead on the property became the clubhouse, which remained in use until 1966 when it was replaced by the present building. (Carol Hila)

CAUGHT IN THE DAISY PATCH, *c.* 1899. This young golfer, a fashionable "Gibson Girl," seems a bit perplexed about how to get her ball back on the green at the Colonia Country Club. Perhaps the gentleman on the left or their caddy will have some sage advice. In 1923 Edward K. Cone, founder of the club, purchased 55 additional acres to expand the original nine-hole golf course to eighteen holes.

COLONIA INN, *c.* 1920. The original section of this house at 477 Colonia Boulevard was built in 1774. An early owner was a Doctor Libby who lived here with his daughter Laura Jean Libby, the author of romance stories published in several newspapers. Later, another owner turned the house into a popular restaurant known for its chicken dinners. Today this historic Colonia landmark remains as a private residence.

Selected Bibliography

Clayton, W. Woodford (ed). *History of Union and Middlesex Counties, New Jersey*. Philadelphia: Everts and Peck, 1882.

Cunningham, John T. *This is New Jersey* (third edition). New Brunswick: Rutgers University Press, 1978.

Dally, Rev. Joseph W. *Woodbridge and Vicinity, The Story of a New Jersey Township*. Lambertville, New Jersey: Hunterdon House, reprinted 1989, originally published 1873.

Fords Yesterday and Today, published in recognition of the New Jersey Tercentenary, 1664–1964.

Jost, Edna Oberlies and Margaret Krewinkel Jost. *An Historical Sampler, 1664–1964—What's Cooking in Woodbridge, New Jersey*. 1964.

Kreger, John. "Woodbridge and Its Clays," *The Independent Leader*, Tercentenary Edition, June 11, 1964.

Newberry, Lida (ed). *New Jersey Guide to its Present and Past*, (new revised edition). New York: Hastings House, 1977.

Wallen, Dick. *Board Track, Guts, Gold and Glory*. Published by the author, 1990.

Wolk, Ruth. *The History of Woodbridge, New Jersey*. Woodbridge, 1970.